DAVID HAMILTON'S

Long and Winding Road

MY LIFE, LOVES AND LESSONS LEARNED

AUSTIN MACAULEY PUBLISHERS™

LONDON • CAMBRIDGE • NEW YORK • SHARJAH

A CIP catalogue record for this title is available from the British Library.

ISBN 9781035860692 (Paperback)
ISBN 9781035860708 (ePub e-book)

www.austinmacauley.com

First Published 2024
Austin Macauley Publishers Ltd®
1 Canada Square
Canary Wharf
London
E14 5AA

THANKS...

To Noel Tyrrel, who set up David Hamilton`s Hotshots Facebook in 2016 as a labour of love, posts all my radio and TV shows on it and has a wonderful library of my work down the years.

To Andy Walmsley, Dave Hall, Alan Jarvie and Junior Coker, for their priceless contributions to the Hotshots Facebook group.

To Kevin Wharram who devised my website davidhamilton.biz

To Lynda Barnett, my most loyal supporter going back to 1963 and for all the lovely letters she has had published in newspapers and magazines.

To Tony Fitzpatrick, my manager (tony@peoplematter.tv)

To Dreena Hamilton for sharing my journey for 40 years and for telling me, "It`s not over until the fat lady sings."

To Walter Stephenson from Austin Macauley, for his work on this *Long and Winding Road*.

Cover photographs: Peter Robertson and Photographs Forever

FOREWORD

T HIS is the remarkable story of a broadcaster whose career spans the lion's share of the lifetime of the radio medium itself.

When David Hamilton's broadcasting journey began, there were just three UK radio stations, FM was a new-fangled thing – and radio audiences easily surpassed those of TV.

An 18-year-old Cliff served as one of his earliest interviewees, a fitting apprenticeship for later conversations with some promising young Beatles.

David has conducted the nation's journey from era to era, playing light orchestral pieces on the radio and then introducing The Rolling Stones on stage; drawing the shutters on the BBC Light Programme and opening the ones which heralded Thames TV.

Now, he remains one of the nation's best recognised voices thanks to a reputation carved out over decades in BBC and commercial radio, where I began working with him over 20 years ago. In the '70s and '80s, it was difficult to find a radio not tuned into his distinctive tones as he broadcast simultaneously each day across BBC Radio 1 and 2. His influence helped to carve out some of the era's most popular music artistes.

On TV too, 'Diddy's' journey ran in parallel to the medium itself as he graduated from dinner-jacketed monochrome announcer to a host of colourful TV shows including Top of The Pops. He served alongside generations of entertainment's biggest names including Ken

Dodd, Benny Hill and Tommy Cooper. And he wound up Lionel Blair and Noele Gordon.

Even as a household name, he's always had time for his listeners and viewers. As this book tells, just a few of them weren't so keen on him – and others craved rather more of his attention than he wisely gave.

You don't devote 65 years to this industry without amassing a wealth of stories from the biggest stars and the most puzzling of colleagues. I'm so pleased David has chosen to write such an honest account of his enviably rich life – from the heart. The undulating journey from his square-bashing days through to rubbing shoulders with the greats.

It's personal too, with David opening up about those who broke his heart and the ones who brought him happiness. The things he got right – and where he messed up.

In an unforgiving media world, long careers are rare. David owes his to the way he has managed his gifts, his energy, his work ethic – and seizing every opportunity. Even when launching his daily show on Boom Radio, aged 82, he insisted on dry runs to make sure all would be well. It was. His listeners are now relishing being able to pick up on the relationship he began with them all those years ago.

As you'll read, he's serious about his work, but never takes himself too seriously – and he's one of the nicest, most positive, most generous, most thoughtful people you could wish to know.

DAVID LLOYD
RADIO HISTORIAN AND MEDIA EXECUTIVE

Life should not be a journey to the grave with the intention of arriving safely in a pretty and well preserved body but rather to skid in broadside in a cloud of smoke, thoroughly used up, totally worn out and loudly proclaiming, "Wow! What a ride!"

HUNTER S. THOMPSON

INTRO

I grew up on a remote farm in Sussex, listening to the stars on the wireless and dreaming of the bright lights. In time I got those bright lights. *Top of the Pops*, TV quiz and game shows, beauty contests. I hosted TV shows in New York and Los Angeles. Back in the UK, I appeared in every town and city, at one time covering 50,000 miles a year on the road. Through a chance meeting, I found a house on the farm of my youth, returning there after more than fifty years, little realising that I would broadcast from my farmhouse, becoming at 85 the oldest person with a daily show on national radio.

CHAPTER 1

To the Farm

M Y father used to say, "It's a good man who knows his own father." Sadly, he didn't. He was born illegitimate in Dublin, circa 1909. The name on his birth certificate was Claude Joseph Desmond, Desmond being his mother Catherine's surname. By the end of World War 1 he and his mother had moved to London along with a maid with a glass eye called Kitty Maloney. Where did the money come from to pay for the maid, let alone a home for Catherine Desmond and her son in London? In the future there would be much speculation that her lover was a wealthy, and maybe even powerful, man. In London, Catherine would meet another wealthy man. Gerald Arthur Pascal Pilditch, known as Peter, owned a chain of kiosks on railway stations dotted around the country. After they married, Claude adopted his name, becoming Claude Pilditch.

He was a bookish boy with a love of words and, not surprisingly, went into journalism, starting on his local paper, the *Wimbledon Boro News*, before transferring to the *West Sussex County Times* in Horsham. It was here at the local tennis club that he met Joyce Hamilton, a pretty farmer's daughter. Joyce was already seeing a Sussex cricketer but Claude eliminated the competition by telling the other man when he visited the farmhouse that Joyce was his fiancée. Premature perhaps, but before long they were married and moved to Manchester where he was taken on as a reporter on the *Daily Mail*. For some reason unknown to me people started calling him Tony, though I believe his by-line was C.J. Pilditch.

Early in the marriage, my mother became pregnant but the child, a girl, was stillborn. I arrived on 10 September 1938, at a maternity home in Whalley Range. The survivor. I went back with my daughter Jane to see the building a few years ago. It is now a Chinese embassy. How things change.

Big changes were underway in the late 1930s. Almost exactly a year after I was born, World War 2 broke out and mass evacuation began. Thousands of children were evacuated from big towns and cities to the countryside. Most stayed with foster families who agreed to take them in but it was decided that my mother and I would move to the farm my grandfather ran in Sussex. My father, as a journalist, may have been in a reserved occupation but

At the farm with Sister Brother

elected to do his bit for his wife, son and country and joined the Army.

The farm was a wonderful place to grow up, roaming the fields with our black and white sheepdog, Scamp, but, as an only child, rather a lonely one – no siblings or friends of my own age. My mother gave me a stuffed monkey who I called Sister Brother: nonbinary decades before that word was even thought of. From an early age, I learned to make my own entertainment.

The farmhouse was quite primitive. Lighting came from paraffin oil lamps. We toasted bread with a large, long fork on the coal fire. There was a pump in the kitchen which brought the water up from a well. With the farm only 30 miles from the South coast, there was fear of invasion. There were huge telegraph poles in the fields to prevent enemy planes from landing and massive concrete blocks on bridges to stop German tanks from crossing the river. The nearest Army camp was just two and a half miles away but the only sign of war we heard was the eerie noise of a doodlebug one night. We cowered under the kitchen table – as if that would make much difference – until we heard the noise cut out when the dreaded bomb landed in a nearby farm. In 1942 we were appalled to hear that a train on a line we some-times used to Guildford had been attacked by a German bomber whose crew opened fire on it as it approached Bramley and Wonersh station, killing eight people. Years later Dr Beeching did what the Germans failed to do and closed the line from Horsham to Guildford completely.

In our remote farmhouse the radio was our window to the world. It brought us all the wonderful variety shows like *ITMA*, *Take It From Here* and *Ray's A Laugh*. *Workers' Playtime* came from a factory somewhere in

Britain – the venue kept secret in case the Nazis bombed it. All the comedians had catchphrases and when we heard them we fell about as though it was the funniest thing we'd ever heard. There was Ken Platt, "I won't take me coat off, I'm not stopping." Rob Wilton, "The day war broke out, my wife said to me…" And, of course, "Can I do you now, Sir?" (Mrs Mopp.) As I grew older, I'd impersonate them at Christmas time to entertain the family. There were the wonderful football commentaries from Raymond Glendenning. What would it be like to be among huge crowds at White Hart Lane or St James's Park, I pondered, when all I saw were cows and a few pigs?

When the time came to go to school, my mother cycled me two and a half miles to the local kindergarten in a basket on the front of her bike and brought me home in the afternoon. On the journey she must have bumped into the soldiers from the local camp. One in particular, a Captain Jack Hall who ran the Quartermaster's Stores, often came to the farm in his Jeep and pitched me a tent I could camp out in the field near the house. Daisy Hare, a land girl, had been allotted to the farm and one of her duties was to milk the cows by hand. In her off time she and my mother went dancing in a local hall known as 'The Sweat Box', not far from the Army camp. Everyone was doing their best to keep their spirits high during the war.

Meanwhile, my father was in Italy, a Corporal fighting with the Royal Hampshire regiment. He had a pretty awful time, shot and hospitalised in Bari. When the war swung in our direction he finished his service in Rome writing for an Army newspaper called *The Crusader*.

At the age of six, I was sent to a boarding school in Billingshurst. It was a convent, 'The Immaculate Heart of Mary', where the nuns were used to teaching girls, but not boys. Because it was wartime a few boys were seconded to the school. If I remember correctly, there were three boys and about 200 girls, odds I was too young to appreciate. The nuns were surprisingly tough, not at all the daughters of God you would expect. I do remember skipping piano lessons – something I regretted in later life when I saw gifted pianists like Tony Hatch entertaining people at parties as they all stood round the piano and sang songs. Looking back, I was far too young to go to boarding school – 'farmed out' might be the right expression.

Back on the farm my grandfather, George Hamilton, struggled through the war years to make ends meet. I still have today the books in which he kept the farm's accounts. They show that by selling milk, heifers and pigs and by harvesting the corn in the autumn, he just about broke even. George was the bailiff, answerable to Dorothy Henderson, a wealthy landowner based in Scotland and only an occasional visitor to Sussex. When she came she stayed in the largest house on the farm, the jewel in the crown. It was so big that as part of the war effort she allowed it to be turned into a boys' boarding school. I remember going there once and for the first time seeing a film. There was a projector and a screen and the film was *The Lady Vanishes* with Margaret Lockwood. I sat there in awe. Afterwards the boys sang 'Camptown Races'.

As well as the cows and pigs, my grandfather had two carthorses, Josh and Diamond, which pulled the farm cart. For a long time he resisted the use of tractors so that the horses would have a job and survive.

My mother loved the farm, it held all her childhood memories, and I'm sure she was not at all unhappy to be back home from Manchester. It was in a beautiful valley with the river Arun running through it and on to the sea at Littlehampton. There was an old mill with a wheel that once ground the corn, a practice that went on until the 1920s. Her brother, my Uncle John Hamilton, saw it in a much more practical way. "You can't live on scenery," he said.

John became a bit of a hero to me. As I got older, he played football with me in the driveway of the farmhouse. He had lots of funny sayings: "When I woke up today I felt like two men. One's dying and the other bugger's dead." Once asked during his childhood to share a bed for the night with his father, he said, "I'd rather sleep with a dead policeman."

So, happy days on the farm. We heard about the horrors of war on the radio and read about them in the newspaper, but it all seemed a long way away. People loved to come and visit us. Dick and Ethel, friends of my mother, drove from their home in New Cross. As they headed south the roads became narrower and narrower until they reached the farm lane. The long and winding road that leads to our door. When they arrived Agnes, my grandmother, would shout "Hooray." She hated it when people left, there was a flat feeling in the air.

Suddenly it was all over. The first time I realised the war had ended was when my father came walking up the long drive to the convent. I was so young when he left for Italy, I would have no memory of what he looked like, but I knew instantly it was him. "Daddy, Daddy," I shouted, and I leaped into his arms. He was home, and now my saviour would take me away from this miserable place and back home to the farm.

Sadly, the welcome he got from my mother was not so warm. Hardly was he home before she told him she had met someone else – yes, Uncle Jack, the Army captain who pitched my tent for me. My father told her he hadn't been entirely celibate in Italy but that was wartime, nobody knew if there would be a tomorrow, but now things were back to normal. "But I'm in love with him," said my mother.

Not quite the hero's welcome he had expected. Through all the horrors of war in Italy what had kept him going was the thought that one day he would return to his loving wife and son, and now that dream was dashed. A story to be repeated many times in World War 2. The irony is not lost on me that while my father, a gentle journalist and undoubtedly a pacifist, was fighting for his life in Italy, Jack, a regular soldier in the Kings Regiment from Liverpool, had a cushy number here organising food and clothing and never heard a shot fired in anger.

Somehow my father talked my mother into trying to make a go of it. Catherine, my father's mother, had recently died and my parents moved into her flat in Raynes Park, near Wimbledon. My father found a job working nights; not ideal, but there was no way they were moving back to Manchester. One evening I was in bed and could hear voices so I got up to investigate. My mother quickly ushered me back to the bedroom, explaining it was a man who had come to read the gas meter. Somehow in the evening glow he seemed familiar.

After about a year at a local school, Dundonald Road, the dreaded news came – I was going back to board-ing school. This time it was to be Kingswood House in Epsom. It was on the train to there from Wimbledon one Sunday evening that my father gave me the news. "Your mother and I are going our separate ways. You will still see us both, but not together."

"But I want to see you together," I said.

"I'm afraid that won't be possible," said my father. "One day you will understand these things and you will realise why."

I'm sure his heart was broken, and now mine was, too. It was a very unhappy boy that returned to Kingswood House that Sunday night. I hated boarding school and before long I was in fights with other boys, though when they put me in the boxing ring, part of the school curriculum, they matched me up with a boy who was much the same size as me but one of the best boxers in the school. I met Peter Gethin again years later when he became a successful racing driver and reminded him of how he knocked eight bells out of me.

While I was at Kingswood House I made my stage debut in a school production of *The Pirates of Penzance*. I told my friends I was playing the Major General, a very grand role. In fact, I was one of the chorus girls, complete with bonnet and false curls and a Dorothy bag. When they spotted me, there was a great deal of mickey-taking from the audience, followed by some very unlady-like gestures from the chorus girl, mainly involving two fingers.

It was quite commonplace for boys to be caned for some perceived misdemeanour, either on the hand or the bottom and one master seemed to derive particular pleasure from it. All we could do was make sure they didn't see us cry.

During the unhappy days at boarding school all I could look forward to was the school holidays, especially visits to my Auntie Gertie. Gertie was my grandmother's sister. Her husband was a bus driver based at Willesden Garage and they lived at Dollis Hill, just a few stops on the tube from Wembley Stadium. Gertie was a speed freak and during the summer would take my cousin, Ian, and me to watch the Wembley Lions speedway team. In the years after the war people were longing for entertainment, and speed and thrills was just what they wanted. Huge crowds – anything up to 80,000 – congregated at Wembley on Thursday nights to watch the motorbike gladiators in action. I can't tell you how thrilling it was for the boy from the farm who saw so few people to be in such a gathering. Everything was magical. The noise of the bikes and the crowd, the smell of methanol – even better when darkness fell and the lights came on. There was extra entertainment in the interval which added to the spectacle. One night, a man called Daredevil Peggy, a war hero with only one leg, climbed a ladder up to a turret way above the crowd and dived down into a vat of water which appeared to be on fire.

After the war everyone was bomb-crazy. The Wembley Lions were the top team and competed in a mainly London league plus Bradford and the Belle Vue Aces from Manchester. Their star rider was Tommy Price, one of my early heroes. Auntie Gertie confessed that when the racing was exciting she wet her knickers. When I was back at boarding school I would ring her and ask, "Did the Lions win? Did Tommy Price get a maximum? Did you wet your knickers?" When she said, "Several times," I knew it had been a good meeting.

My father rarely talked about his time in Italy, not wanting to re-live it. One story I do remember him telling was of the time he was lying injured on a stretcher in a trench. Above him were two stretcher bearers. Suddenly, a shell struck nearby. He looked up and realised the stretcher bearers were dead. How frightening, knowing the people who would carry him to safety were now gone.

Meanwhile, Jack Hall was rewarded for his heroic task of organising food and clothing on the home front by being promoted to the rank of Major and posted to a series of desk jobs around the country. The first was in Dorchester and he and my mother rented a lovely thatched cottage in the pretty village of Osmington near Weymouth. When I went to stay with them in the summer of 1947 they seemed idyllically happy.

During the war my father had undergone another name change and became Bill Pilditch. Army humour, no doubt. Bill Pil. After my parents' divorce Bill met a woman called Delia Lucock. She had a gap in her teeth and a large bottom and I couldn't see how he fancied her. She often wore around her neck a fur stole with a fox's head on it. Quite revolting. She spoke in a 'Hyacinth Bouquet' voice, pronouncing the 'h' in 'where' and 'when'. My father wasn't very good on his own, and before long Bill and Del were married and moved into a council flat in Gap Road, Wimbledon.

Just a few weeks into the marriage, a delivery man arrived at the door. "Are you by any chance Mrs Delilah Piedish?"

"No, I'm not," she said and slammed the door.

With Delia I acquired a large number of step relations. She had three sisters. Reenie was married to a vicar in Berkshire and had two daughters. We didn't see much of them. Peggy had a son called Robin. He was the adored only son in the family. Like me, he was at boarding school and great things were expected of him. The youngest sister, Gay, never married but appears to have conducted a long affair with a married man. Delia's brother, Percy, was a very successful businessman. Apparently, he'd made a lot of money during the war and lived in a large house in West Byfleet with his wife Mab and daughter Valerie. Not long after Bill and Del's wedding we were invited there for Christmas. I'd never imagined such a grand place, with lots of bedrooms and a large garden. When Percy drove Bill back to Wimbledon after the holiday, my father asked him to drop him at Wimbledon station. "No, I'll take you to the door," said Percy. My father insisted on getting out at the station. Embarrassed about the council flat, perhaps, or maybe he wanted to drop into one of the three pubs near the station.

After the idyllic summer in Osmington, Major Jack Hall, whose real names were John Thomas (ahem), was posted to Warlingham in Surrey and then central London. This posting lasted longer and he and my mother moved into a flat in Ranelagh Gardens Mansions, next to Putney Bridge station. By 1948 my parents were just four miles away from each other, though they never spoke. My mother's flat was pretty basic. There were two bedrooms. The bath was in the kitchen covered by a table top. To take a bath, someone had first to remove the table top and its contents. Consequently, no one bathed as often as they should. For the rest of my life I've always appreciated a bath and taken one nearly every day.

One thing Jack and my father had in common was a love of football. My father was a Chelsea supporter and took me to my first match at Stamford Bridge. I didn't like the ground much. There was a greyhound track around the pitch and as a young boy I was a long way from the action. Jack was a Liverpudlian and supported the Reds from his home city. When they played at Fulham, the ground was just a short stroll along the Thames through Bishop's Park. At Craven Cottage I could stand behind the goal close to the action. Though Chelsea and Fulham were my local teams, my favourite player turned out for neither club.

I first saw pictures of Sam Bartram when his team, Charlton Athletic, beat Burnley to win the FA Cup at

Wembley in 1947. I first saw him in action playing for Charlton at Fulham the following season. With his green jersey and red hair he stood out from the other players on the pitch. He was a spectacular showman, dubbed England's finest uncapped goalkeeper – uncapped probably because of his tendency to play to the crowd. He was something rare even in those days, a player popular at opposition clubs who received an ovation from the crowd wherever he played.

Inspired by Sam, I played in goal for the under-11s football team at Kingswood House. A review in the school magazine said… "David Pilditch was the most promising player in the Under-11 team. With a few more inches he could be a good player." With a father who was 5ft 4, it should have been obvious to me that I was not going to be a goalkeeper.

In 1948 I persuaded my father to buy me a new table football game called Subbuteo. It was a game that millions of boys would play in the post-war years. It came with a pitch and goals and we started off with my father's team, Chelsea, and my hero Sam Bartram's team, Charlton. We later added my local team, Fulham, and other teams chosen by their variety of colours, like Reading with their blue and white hoops and Blackburn with their quartered shirts. After a while we developed three leagues, each with five teams, two managed by my father and me and one by Delia. On match days the third person would be the referee, complete with whistle. Poor Delia. She had little interest in football and was hopeless at the game but, bless her, she did her best. After a while I started bringing out a *Subbuteo Monthly* magazine, initially written in exercise books and then typed on the Empire Aristocrat typewriter my father bought me.

I taught myself to type and the magazine contained the

month's results and league tables as well as features and photographs which were pasted in. These I got from newspapers and magazines and Agnes, my grandmother, weighed in by sending me football pictures she saw in the *Daily Mirror*.

To play the matches the pitch had to be fixed to the dining room table with tin tacks, leaving great holes around the side of it. To enhance the matchday experience I played records on my father's radiogram in the warm up before kick-off. Naturally, as well as the three leagues we had a Cup competition. For the Cup Final in May – a week after the real Cup Final – some family members and friends were invited to form a crowd in the flat and I rigged up a microphone in Bill and Del's bedroom so I could announce the teams to them – a taste

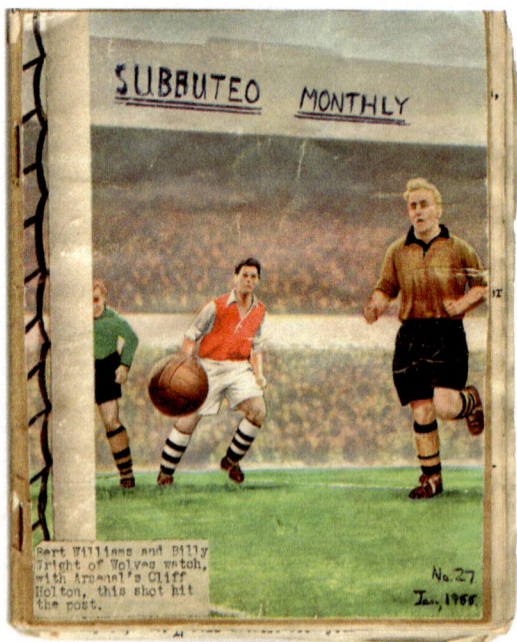

Cover of Subbuteo Monthly

of things to come? And, of course, there was a cup for the winning team.

The problem with the weekday matches was that my father was always late back from the pub, so kick-off was delayed and more records had to be played to keep the imaginary crowd entertained. Poor Delia – an expression you may hear so much that you might think her first name was Poor – would then have timing problems with dinner which she could only serve when the match was over and the pitch removed.

My father spent a great deal of time at the pub and alcohol rapidly became something that dominated his life. Had he been like this before the war, I wondered, or was it exacerbated by his wartime experiences and the breakup of his marriage? Family albums show that the war changed so many things in my parents' lives. Before

Subbuteo Cup Final winner with my father, May, 1952

the war there were sports cars, houses and always dogs. After the war my father never drove again, they both lived in pokey flats and there were no dogs anymore.

My father had a number of jobs after the war. For a while he was the PR man for the Grosvenor House Hotel in London. There he would get me the autographs of the famous stars who stayed there, like the Australian Invincibles cricket team, including Don Bradman. When he started there, the Head Waiter asked him what his favourite tipple was. "Whisky," said my father.

"You'll be entertaining a lot," said the waiter. "If you want a whisky, ask for whisky. If you want something watered down, ask for a Scotch."

On occasions when the waiter offered, "Would you like a Scotch, sir?" my father would reply, "No, I don't want a Scotch. I want a bloody whisky."

When that job didn't last long, he found another one running the London night news desk of the *Sydney Morning Herald*, wiring stories of interest to Australians from the offices in Reuter House in Fleet Street. It meant unsociable hours but, as he worked alone in the office, he could come and go as he liked and he worked out a little routine where he could drink round the clock. It began with a visit to the Cock pub at the top of Fleet Street, near the Law Courts, which opened an hour earlier than the others, at five o'clock. He'd pop out to the Punch near the office in the evening and when his shift finished at 2 a.m. he'd look in at a pub in Smithfield Market which stayed open through the night for the market workers. Originally, the *Morning Herald* laid on a car to take him home but then he persuaded them to give him the money and he'd make his own way. This involved walking over Waterloo Bridge, often in freezing weather, and catching the first morning train back to Wimbledon and a walk of a mile or so from there back to the flat. I'd have opted for the car every time, but we're all different.

Delia had a good job. She was secretary to the Chairman of the United Dominions Trust in Pall Mall. By the time my father arrived home, she had left for work. Ships that pass in the night. A difficult marriage. Poor Delia.

My father seemed to be drinking more and more. One evening, waiting for him to return home to play the Subbuteo match I'd been building up to, I'd been peering out of my bedroom window, watching the 77A buses pulling up at the bus stop across the road. At last I spotted him walking towards the flat. Next thing he was sitting on the low wall outside getting undressed. I ran out. "Dad, Dad, what are you doing?"

"Get off me," he said. "I'm going to bed." Seeing my father like that was very distressing.

He was two people. Sober he was just the gentlest, nicest man anyone could wish to know. But, as I worked out later, he didn't like himself like that. He liked to be the life and soul of the party – the larger-than-life, witty character, singing old Irish songs like 'The Spinning Wheel' by Delia Murphy. He knew all the Irish words that didn't mean a thing to me. He was a great joke-teller and most of his jokes were near the bone. Some I remember to this day.

He told the one about two hookers comparing their takings at the end of the day.

"I made three pounds seven shillings and sixpence."

"Who gave you the sixpence?"

"They all did."

For a long time my father resisted having a television in the flat but he did have a radiogram and he did like to collect records that were unusual and sometimes funny – like Peter Sellers and Sophia Loren and 'Goodness

Gracious Me'. He liked to play Kay Starr and 'Rock 'n' Roll Waltz' and Les Paul and Mary Ford with 'How High the Moon'. When he was out, which was a lot, I listened to the radio. By this time I'd outgrown the BBC, which was into big band music. Like the rest of my generation, I wanted to hear rock 'n' roll and for that we tuned in at night to Radio Luxembourg. The signal was awful because it was bounced across the sea from the Grand Duchy of Luxembourg but we sat there twiddling the knob of the radio to get a better reception. It was Luxembourg that introduced a new job description, disc-jockey, and the star turn was Pete Murray. He was witty and his programmes were fun. I listened to him at night and hung on to his every word. When I saw a picture of him in *FAB 208* magazine, I thought what a glamorous existence he had – horse-riding and answering his fan mail by day and playing records at night. Radio was such a big part of my childhood. It's not surprising that it would be a big part of my adult life.

My mother on Wimbledon Common

CHAPTER 2

To The Valley

I F life is lonely for an only child, it's even more so for an only child from a broken home. When my two years at boarding school were mercifully over I went to a co-ed school in Wimbledon called The Ridgeway and divided my week between my mother's flat in Fulham and my father's in Wimbledon. When I passed my 11-plus I won a place at Glastonbury Road Grammar School on the St Helier estate in Surrey. On the days when I travelled from my mother's it was an eight-mile journey, involving two bus routes.

An even longer journey was the one I took to see my hero Sam Bartram play at Charlton's ground, The Valley. It meant a tube to Charing Cross and then on by train to Charlton. A walk down Floyd Road from the station took me past Sam's sports outfitters shop, Sam Bartram & Co. He was never there on matchdays but I'd pop in and buy pictures of the players which I would paste into *Subbuteo Monthly*. Ones of Sam I'd put in scrapbooks I kept of his career and called Sam Bartram's Goalkeeping Books.

The ground was in a huge bowl with terracing that went on forever. The biggest crowd recorded there was over 80,000. Charlton had a good team; the football was exciting, with five forwards and lots of goals.

I liked to stand on the railings behind the goal as near to my hero as I could get. When there was an attack the crowd would surge forward to get a better view of the action. One Saturday afternoon near to my 13th birthday I felt someone pressed close to me with something hard between the cheeks of my bottom. After a while I felt the person's hand fiddling with my fly buttons. I froze in fear, not understanding what was happening. When the match was over I walked up the hill to Charlton station in a daze. As I boarded the crowded train I found standing next to me a revolting old man in a beret who was staring at me. This, I assumed, must be my assailant. I turned away from him. A couple of stations down the line he said, "This is where I get off," and tried to grab my hand. I pulled away, hanging on tightly to the strap above me. When I got home I tried to make sense of what had happened to me that afternoon. No one then had heard the word paedophile.

Nothing would stop me getting my fix of watching my football hero, so the next time I went to The Valley I stood behind the goal at the other end. A few weeks later I was travelling on the 93 bus from Putney Bridge to Morden on my way to Glastonbury Road school. I sat in the front window seat behind the driver. A man came to sit next to me and I found his leg unnecessarily close to mine.

"Would you like to see some pictures?" he said.

I thought they might be pictures of footballers so I took them from him.

"Hold them down," he said.

When I saw them, I realised why he didn't want anyone sitting behind to see them. They were pictures of naked men doing disgusting things to each other. I quickly handed them back. I pushed past him and went to sit at the back near the conductor. *My God,* I thought, *how many of these monsters are there around?* After that

I never took the bus again. Instead, I cycled eight miles from Fulham to St Helier in the morning. One afternoon on the homeward journey in pouring rain, a motorist knocked me off my bike and I finished up having stitches in my leg in Nelson Hospital. Anything was better than taking the 93 bus.

I did see the man in the beret again. I went with some friends to see Charlton playing at Arsenal, and there he was leaning up against a boy on the railings. I told my friends about him. We went down, tapped him on the shoulder and said, "Oi, mister. Leave that kid alone." He scurried off into the crowd. I wonder how many boys that wretched man molested.

When I see pictures of me in the school football team before and after that assault I see an enormous change. I see the time that a boy changed into a man.

I was aware of that change as well when my father, Delia, my step-cousin Robin and I took a holiday at Walton-on-the-Naze in Essex, staying in a beach hut that was owned by Delia's family. It was late in the summer season, most holidaymakers, including Robin, went home and business on the pier was slack. The chap running the dodgems let me have some free goes, presumably on the principle that with one person on there, there was a chance that he would get at least one more. At last she arrived, an attractive young woman, possibly just a little older than me. My first real encounter with the opposite sex, and we literally bumped into each other, ending up on the cliffs where we got to know each other a little better. It was at that moment I realised that, despite efforts to lead me to other persuasions, I was definitely attracted to women. We swapped telephone numbers and when the holidays were over I cycled over 30 miles across London to join her and her father for Sunday lunch at their home at Waltham Cross. It was there that I learned the hard lesson of holiday romances. Away from the dodgem cars and the sea breezes, all the magic had gone.

Looking back now, I realise that was the only holiday either of my parents took me on. Most summers my father and Delia would go to Jersey for a fortnight. My father loved it, partly because he could get his fags and booze duty-free. I never dreamed of going abroad.

My one holiday over, it was time to rekindle my interest in football and I was really enjoying my time in the school team. Having given up my ambition to be a goalkeeper, I'd switched to playing on the wing, which suited me much better. We had a good team and every season we won the St Helier district league. Two of the team, John Shears and Brian Hardey, went on to play for Wimbledon, who were then in the Isthmian League. I got to play for the district team but when I had a trial at

Far left, front row in Glastonbury Road Grammar School, St. Helier Cup winners, 1955

Wimbledon, whose ground at Plough Lane was just a few hundred yards from my father's flat, I didn't get taken on.

If I wasn't going to have a career playing football, the next best thing was to write about it. Every week a magazine called *Soccer Star* would land on the mat of

26 February 1956 edition of Soccer Star, *with a front-page article by 'David Pilditch' (DH)*

my mother's flat, delivered by the newsagent at Putney Bridge station. I devoured it from cover to cover. In the close season in the summer of 1954, with all the wisdom of a 15-year-old schoolboy, I reckoned they might be short of material so I sent them an article which, to my surprise, they published with the caption... "David Pilditch, who submitted this article, is one of our old and regular readers". Old and regular? Certainly regular.

Everything was done by letters in those days so I wrote to them again, asking if they would be interested in my writing a weekly column for them. Again to my surprise they wrote back saying that they would. As they were a London-based magazine, they wanted me to write every week a report on a provincial team for which they would pay me two guineas. Two guineas to a schoolboy seemed a fortune. So at the age of 16, I became a columnist on *Soccer Star*. Every week I would set off to a London ground, mainly the local clubs, Fulham and Chelsea; Charlton, of course; and occasionally somewhere else like West Ham or Arsenal. I didn't ask for a press pass and they didn't offer one. I paid through the turnstile like everyone else. My father would pick up a copy of *Soccer Star* in Fleet Street and make little corrections or suggestions in the margin. This I regarded as sacrilege, though looking back now I realise it was priceless advice.

Over in Fulham there was bad news. Jack was suddenly taken ill. I can't say I liked him much. He had a regimental attitude and was hot on discipline, always telling me to polish my shoes. The one good thing about him was that he did take me to some football matches and in the autumn of 1954 we went to Wembley stadium to see England play the Rest of the World. Not long after, he was taken to the Army hospital at Woolwich where he died suddenly at the age of 50. The day of the funeral was one of the saddest of my life. Because we had no car my mother's friends, Dick and Ethel, drove us from their home in New Cross. I'd always assumed Jack and my mother were married – I'm sure she told me they were – but on the journey to Woolwich she told us that Jack was still married to someone else and that his wife and son would be at the ceremony. It was a regimental funeral and we sat in the car in a lay-by watching the gun carriages pass and then the car with the mourners. "That must be his wife," said my mother. "And that's his son." When everybody had left we walked up the little hill in the cemetery, found Jack's grave and my mother laid her flowers on it. What a sad and abrupt end to their ten years or so together.

Jack left everything to his wife, leaving my mother penniless in her early 40s. Once she got over the shock she got a job as a salesgirl, selling women's clothing at Richards Shops in Putney High Street. She was so good at it that she eventually became a travelling manageress, then spent a long time managing the Richards store in Tunbridge Wells.

These were tough times for my mother. Her parents were growing old and tired. It became increasingly difficult for them to run the farm and break even financially. Dorothy Henderson, the owner, kept it going out of loyalty to them and all their hard work over the years. My mother and I went back as often as we could. The journey there, which today would take not much more than an hour, then took the best part of a day, carrying our suitcases on the tube from Putney Bridge to Wimbledon; then the train to Horsham; the Aldershot and District bus to Rudgwick, followed by a two and a half mile walk along the long and winding road to the farm. In 1956 the decision was made that the farm would be sold and my grandparents moved into a house in Horsham where they were like fish out of water. It wasn't long before they passed away. My mother lost her partner and both her parents within a short space of time.

On days at Fulham I played football with Michael, the boy from the flat above, in Bishops Park. Michael was a little younger than me and his mother, I couldn't help noticing, was an attractive woman, probably in her early thirties. Back then footballs had bladders which you had to inflate. One day she was pumping the bladder up while thrusting it into the case. "I'm very good at pushing," she said, looking at me. I blushed furiously – I was a serial blusher. *Was she trying to tell me something?* I asked myself in my schoolboy way. Sometime later the family moved to Stoneleigh in Surrey and I cycled down to see Michael for a kickabout. When I got there he was out but his mother offered to show me round the house. We spent an inordinate amount of time in the spare bedroom, I thought. On a second visit she said, "I'm not sure if you come to see Michael or to see me." Cue more blushing. "I come to see you both," I said, coming up with the polite answer.

I never went back again. I was afraid the blushing would give me away to Michael or his father. What an idiot. She could have taught me all I needed to know about women and saved me all the stumbling, fumbling mistakes I would make in the future. Or maybe I mis-read the signs and could have made a fool of myself. I will never know.

As word spread at Glastonbury Road about my writing for *Soccer Star*, Mr Hawkins, the English teacher who also ran the football team, decided to revive the school magazine and asked me to edit it. So by 1955 I was editing and writing *The Glastonian* and *Subbuteo Monthly*, as well as writing for *Soccer Star* and writing and compiling my Sam Bartram scrapbooks. Although I was good at English -something I had inherited from my father – I was dreadful at things like algebra and geometry and especially woodwork, all things I just knew I would never need in my life. In such lessons I was badly behaved and disruptive in school. A lot of the other boys were, too, but Mr Hawkins – not entirely blinded by my talents – said I had a great future as a gang boss. I wonder now, was I really that bad? And if so, what was it that made me so wilful?

I left Glastonbury Road aged 17 with three A levels – in English Language, English Literature and French. I could have got more if I hadn't mucked around so much.

At Christmas 1955, the Wimbledon Subbuteo league played its last game and I brought out the 39th and final edition of *Subbuteo Monthly*. Now it was time to get a job. The first logical step was to see if there was a staff job going at *Soccer Star*. I made an appointment to see the Editor at his office at Cheapside with a view through the window of St Paul's Cathedral. When I got there I was astounded to see how untidy everything was with photos strewn all over the floor. They were astounded to find out how young their 'old and regular' reader was. I didn't get the job. Not only did I not get a job on the staff, but they dropped my column as well. That seemed a bit tough. Couldn't they see that if I could write like that as a teenager, what potential might I have for the future? Or were they embarrassed in case people found out that one of their writers was a schoolboy? A hard lesson early in life.

One of my last articles was a two-page spread about Sam Bartram on his 42nd birthday in January 1956. Two months later he retired suddenly to become the manager of York City. This football superman lasted much longer in the top division of English football than most players and played more times for Charlton than any other player in the history of the club. He would have made even more appearances had not the war put paid to six seasons of league football. His retirement meant the end of my trips to Charlton. From now on any football would be watched at my local club, Fulham. Today a statue of Sam Bartram stands outside the ground at The Valley, confirming that my boyhood hero was indeed a great man. It is nine feet tall. That's how I remember him.

After leaving school, I was out of work for two months. My father was probably fed up with me lounging around the house and told me, "You must get a job – any job." He suggested I go to the Fleet Street Youth Employment Bureau. I knew that independent television was the exciting new medium, so when I got there I asked if they had any jobs for writers at ITV. They said "No" but there was a vacancy for an office boy, not what I wanted at all. When I got home and told my father he said, "Take it. You'll be on the inside, you'll meet people. You never know what it might lead to."

So I took my first job at ATV in their offices in Kingsway as a messenger boy, collecting and delivering the mail for the good and the great like Lew Grade and Val Parnell for £3-17s and 6d a week. This I found quite difficult because it involved knocking on doors and walking into crowded offices. More blushing, I'm afraid. How foolish. As if anybody could care less about a humble little messenger boy. As a young man I was quite highly strung. I had the opposite syndrome from Prince Andrew. I sweated a lot. To celebrate my new job, my father bought me an £8 suit from Hepworth's and in no time a white ring appeared under the armpit. As I could only afford one suit, my mother had to sew in sweat pads.

There weren't many people of my age working at ATV but there was one, a girl called Beryl, working in the duplicating department, printing off people's scripts. She was a petite brunette, very attractive I thought, and I summoned up the courage to ask her out. Our dates were fairly modest as neither of us had much money. It was impossible for me to invite her to my mother or father's flats and so some weekends we would stay at her parents' house in Goff's Oak in Hertfordshire. This involved a long train journey to Cuffley and then a long walk from the station. Like all teenagers, we loved our music and on Saturday nights we watched the first TV pop show, *6.5 Special*, hosted by Pete Murray. We went to the cinema and loved Debbie Reynolds in *Tammy*. The first record I bought her was 'Love Letters in the Sand' by Pat Boone. Very romantic. We went to see Tommy Steele in *The Duke Wore Jeans* and I bought his record 'Butterfingers' on an old 78. On the way home I dropped it and it smashed to pieces. How apt. We decided to go to Brighton and book into a hotel. As Smith was too obvious a name, when we booked in we called ourselves Robinson. She was Mrs Robinson before Simon and Garfunkel invented her.

After a few months on my rounds at ATV I got talking one day to Harold Jamieson, head of the script department. "You seem like a bright boy," he said. "What do you want to do?"

When I told him I wanted to write, he asked me what I had written. I told him about *Soccer Star*. "Bring your cuttings in so I can see them," he said. As luck would have it, I had an article published that week in *TV Times* which he saw. A couple of days later he told me, "I may have something for you soon."

One day he called me into his office and told me there was great excitement that one of his writers, Tessa Diamond, had created ITV's first soap, *Emergency Ward 10*, and would be leaving to write the series. This left a vacancy for a continuity script-writer, writing scripts for the station's in-vision announcers – Peter Cockburn, Arthur Adair and Shaw Taylor in London and Pat Astley and Jean Morton in the Midlands. He was prepared to take me on as a trainee writer for three months. He expressed to me the importance of the scripts. "Advertisers pay an enormous amount of money for a 30-second commercial. You have the same amount of time to sell our programmes and make sure more people are watching us than the BBC." (There were just two channels, BBC and ITV.) ATV certainly weren't paying me a lot of money but the £8 a week was a big improvement on what I was getting in the mail room. Six months after joining ATV and a month before my 18th birthday I was writing my first television scripts. And three months on from that Jamieson, who was an ex-actor and inclined to be dramatic, tapped me on the shoulder and said, "I now dub thee fully-fledged writer." My money went up to £16 a week.

Jamie, as we all called him, was writing a film series called *Portrait of A Star* which went out on ITV on Sunday nights after *The Jack Jackson Show*, narrated by the actor John Fitzgerald. The programme featured a different film star each week with clips from his or her career and appraisal of their acting ability. While Jamie was on holiday, he asked me to write two episodes and told me the subjects would be Marlon Brando and Henry Fonda. If I was writing about footballers it would have been easier. I didn't know much about actors and I was a little young to assess how good their acting was, but I threw myself into it and did the best I could. It involved spending a couple of days at the RCA studios in Hammersmith, watching their films and choosing seven or eight self-contained clips that showed them at their best. When the first show came to air, my mother invited some friends round to her flat in Fulham to watch it on her black and white television set. At the end of the show my credit came up on the screen... Script by David Pilditch. "That's my boy," she said proudly.

All was going well with my script-writing when a buff envelope dropped on the mat at Ranelagh Gardens Mansions, telling me I was due to be called up for National Service and asking which branch I favoured – the Army, Navy or Air Force – and whether I preferred a home posting or one abroad. I suspected that whatever one asked for, they would give you something else. Whichever they came up with, I knew it was going to interrupt my new-found career and my relationship with Beryl and that I was going to spend two years doing something I had absolutely no interest in.

I had heard that the RAF seconded two servicemen to the British Forces Network radio station near Cologne in Germany. The one thing that could save the two years being a complete waste of time would be if I could get to work there, so I wrote 'RAF and Abroad' on my form. I'd already told my old school friends that I wanted to be a disc-jockey, and they laughed at me. "What, you with your sarf London accent? How are you going to do that when all the people on the wireless talk posh?" To find the answer I hired a Grundig tape recorder from a shop in Tottenham Court Road. It was a great, heavy thing with spools. I lugged it home, read articles from newspapers into it and played them back, trying to get rid of the rough edges of my voice.

A second buff envelope arrived, confirming that I had been drafted into the Royal Air Force and giving me a date to report to RAF Cardington in Bedfordshire to be kitted out. I immediately wrote to Ian Woolf, the Station Director at BFN, telling him of my work at ATV, and asking him if he could persuade the RAF to post me to Butzweilerhof near Cologne. He replied that, as a civilian, he had no influence over postings but that if I was able to get there, he would be pleased to see me.

I'm not sure how it came about but I was booked to compere the Surrey Skiffle Championships at the Granada, Sutton in Surrey, not far from my old school. The Granadas were big cinemas – this one held two and a half thousand – and often they put on live stage shows as well as movies. Skiffle was the big music at the time and on Sunday nights in Sutton local groups competed against each other before the big film. My parents came to see my stage debut, though neither knew the other was there. Beryl whisked my mother up to the circle while my father and Delia were towards the back of the stalls, unseen from the balcony. After our little show they all settled back and watched the powerful drama, *The Bridge on the River Kwai*. When the film was over, Beryl made sure they didn't meet up on the way out. Heaven forbid.

As 1957 drew to a close, I was a man on a mission. That mission was to get to Germany and the British forces radio station. However I did it, it had to be done.

CHAPTER 3

Germany Calling

I said a tearful Goodbye to Beryl at St Pancras station, then it was a gloomy train ride to Bedford. Two years is a long time when you're nineteen, and it all seemed so pointless. There was no war so what were we doing? (Three years later National Service was abolished.) When I got to Cardington I got my uniform – probably somebody else's recycled – and was given a number and a rank, 5055032. You never forget it, and have to say it every time you turn up for a pay parade, "5055032 LAC Pilditch, sir." Then salute and click your heels. For that they gave me £1-17-6d a week.

In no time I was off to Bridgnorth, near Wolverhampton for square-bashing. This involved marching, training over obstacle courses and learning to fire guns. It was here that we came into contact with creatures known as Corporals. They were almost without exception ignorant bully boys who enjoyed the power that two stripes gave them to bully new recruits and make them feel like worthless pieces of dirt. This was done to remove any iota of pride or individualism from airmen and turn them into robots. In particular they picked on Teddy Boys who were feared to be the most rebellious. The Corporals were known for their witty repartee. "Am I 'urtin you airman? I ought to be. I'm standin on your 'ead."

One said to me one day, "Airman, there's a wee in your hat?"

"How do you mean, Corporal?" I asked.

He snatched it off my head and threw it away. "Wee," he shouted. "Now go and get it." Very droll.

They liked to insult you and then have you repeat the insult. "Airman, you look like a sack of shit tied up with a piece of string in the middle. What do you look like?"

Airman *(in little voice)*: "A sack of shit."

"A sack of shit, what?"

"A sack of shit, Corporal." You had to be careful not to say just "Shit Corporal" or you'd be in big trouble.

One member of our squadron was a man called Malcolm Fancey, His father owned Fancey Films in Wardour Street. Malcolm spoke with a public school accent and was clearly a cut above the rank of Leading Aircraftman. A Sergeant stuck a baton in his stomach and said, "Airman, there's an idiot at the end of this baton."

Fancey looked him in the eye and said, "Sergeant, I can assure you it's not at my end." Cue stifled laughter.

I've always hated guns and felt the man who invented them should have been shot. They were lethal in the hands of rookies who'd never seen one before. At shooting practice someone missed the target but shot a cow in a neighbouring field, causing enormous animosity between the farmer and the RAF.

After a few days at Bridgnorth it was my turn to see the careers officer, who asked what I wanted to do. I told him the only thing that would stop this two years being a complete waste of time would be if I could get to the forces radio station in Germany. So he made me a wireless operator, listening to Morse code. His idea of a joke, I suppose. I could imagine him laughing about it with his colleagues in the officers' mess. "I had this squaddie in today who wanted to get into radio – so I made him a wireless operator."

"Nice one, Cyril. Have another gin and tonic."

After two months of square-bashing, my next posting was to RAF Compton Bassett in Wiltshire to do a wireless operators' course, learning Morse code. When I got there I was delighted to find there was a billet that housed a closed-circuit radio station that broadcast to the camp. At the first opportunity I strolled across there and introduced myself to the two corporals who ran it, John Dightam and Adrian Irish Malone. When I told them about my script-writing background, they regarded me as a find and immediately gave me a record show. The soundproofing in the studio consisted of egg boxes on the wall. It was here that I did my first radio show early in 1958 to a small but captive audience. Next door to the studio was a lavatory that bore the notice 'DO NOT FLUSH TOILET WHILE RED LIGHT IS ON'. The red light was wired to the microphone and it came on while the mic was live. They didn't want the sound of a flushing toilet while someone was On Air. It could sound like someone taking the piss.

One day, John Dightam came in with the exciting news that some of our programmes would be heard beyond the confines of the camp and that selected shows would be sent by tape to be played on Radio Djibouti. We all waited anxiously to hear if our shows would be selected. When they were, they were preceded by the voice of the continuity announcer saying, "This is CFN, the Compton Forces Network. This programme is also being heard by listeners to Radio Djibouti." I doubt if at the time many of us had a clue where Djibouti was but we felt it was the beginning of our voices being heard beyond the confines of our small camp. The billet had a nice little green room where we all sat around, away from the other troops, drinking tea and talking about our broadcasting dreams for when our time in the forces was up. Many of those dreams would come true. Adrian Malone and John Dightam would forge careers in television. Dave Eastwood, another presenter at CFN, would be a late starter in radio. After working as a lay preacher, he became a DJ on Radio Luxembourg in his thirties. It was Dightam and Malone who suggested I change my name for broadcasting purposes. "Pilditch isn't an easy name for listeners to get," they said. "They may get it wrong." The obvious choice was to adopt my mother's name and my middle name and become David Hamilton.

At Compton Bassett I was promoted to the dizzy heights of Senior Aircraftman. I hated the Morse code. The dah dah dah dit dit dits did my head in. One colleague of ours, John Spence, worked his ticket. He told us, "I'm going to see the medical officer today, and after that I'll be going home." Sure enough, after the meeting he changed into his civilian clothes and was on his way. "How did you do it?" we asked, highly impressed.

"I kept shaking my head, frothing at the mouth and going Dah dah dah dit dit dit, and he said, 'Get that man out of here'." I have to say I was envious. The thought of getting home, seeing Beryl and going back to my job at ATV was very tempting, but my experience at CFN had made me all the more determined to get to BFN in Germany.

Our next move was to RAF Wythall near Birmingham for an advanced wireless operator's course, basically de-coding Russian transmissions. We weren't there long before I learned that we would be doing that – not in Germany, as I had hoped – but at RAF Digby in Lincolnshire. I made an appointment to see the Commanding

Officer at Wythall and told him of the correspondence I had with Ian Woolf, of the opportunity that awaited me in Cologne and of the importance in my life of my posting being changed to Germany. I'm not sure where that confidence and determination came from because in our National Service we were all made to feel worthless, just a number. I don't remember the C.O.'s name and I can't recall what I said to persuade him that I should go to a different camp from anyone else. I didn't get a chance to thank him, but he made a decision that gave me a career that would last for over sixty years. While the rest of the squadron went to the wilds of Lincolnshire, I was on a troop ship from Harwich to the Hook of Holland, onwards by train to Cologne and thence to RAF Butzweilerhof. Anyone who knows how the services work will know that things like that just don't happen. Apart from anything else, there was the cost and the paperwork involved in sending one airman on a solo trip.

I had been very lucky and I was determined to make the most of it. No sooner was I in Germany than I contacted Ian Woolf. "Do you remember my letter? I'm here." I made an appointment to see him, took the bus to Cologne, followed by a long uphill walk to the BFN studios at 61 Parkstrasse in the suburb of Marienburg.

They were situated in two large houses that had been requisitioned by the British after the Second World War. One housed the studios and record library, the other some offices and two bedrooms which I learned were for service personnel who were working there.

In the years after the war the British Forces Network had studios dotted around the world in outposts like Hong Kong, Cyprus and Aden. Germany was the one nearest to home and the one most often featured in *Family Favourites*, the show we all listened to at Sunday lunchtime. It was said to be the only radio show that had its own smell. When you heard the stirring theme – 'With A Song In My Heart' by Andre Kostelanetz – at noon on Sunday you could smell the roast beef and Yorkshire pudding that was cooking in millions of homes across the country. It was also the subject of a radio romance. Jean Metcalfe was the host in London, Cliff Michelmore in Cologne. They fell in love with each other's voices and eventually married. To think his chat-up line was, "What's the weather like in London, Jean?"

Family Favourites was the jewel in the crown at BFN. It got such a huge audience on a Sunday lunchtime that a play on it almost ensured a record would be a hit. Because the BBC didn't really play rock 'n' roll, lots of recording artists came out to Cologne to get their records played via the German end.

I walked into the impressive hallway and was shown into Ian Woolf's office. "It's timely that you have arrived here," he said. "I need someone to read the football results." Because I loved football that was right up my street. I knew it was all about inflection… 'Chelsea 1, FULHAM 2'. (Dream on.) And that's how I began early in 1959. After a few weeks of doing that, I said to Ian one day, "All this music you are playing, like Bing Crosby and Peggy Lee, is fine for the officers, but the troops want rock 'n' roll."

"How do you know?" he asked.

"Because I'm a troop."

I'm not sure he knew what rock 'n' roll was but he said, "I'll give you a show on Sunday afternoons, and we'll see how it goes."

In those days shows had names and I wanted to call mine *Hi There!* He thought that was a bit Americanised but agreed to *Hey There!* Thus in the spring of '59 I launched my career of rock 'n' roll disc-jockey, broadcasting the music of Little Richard, Jerry Lee Lewis and Elvis Presley, who was doing his National Service in the US Army at the same time at Friedburg near Frankfurt. The troops loved having something that at last was aimed at them. Because he was embarrassed about transmitting this heathen music, Ian Woolf followed the show with a speech by the BFN Padre so that he could cleanse the sins of the troops for listening to rock 'n' roll.

The studios were remarkably modern, with the best German equipment and DJs actually playing their own records – self-opping as it was known, a practice that didn't come to the BBC until nearly ten years later. We were told not to fraternise with the German staff, an edict I ignored completely. The war had ended nearly fifteen years ago, this was a new beginning, and they seemed like very decent people. On my 21st birthday they took me to a club in Cologne where I unwittingly became part of the cabaret act. On stage was a magician with a bell tent and an assistant clad in a bikini. He was looking for a volunteer from the audience and my colleagues pushed

In the BFN studio, 1959

the birthday boy forward. "Ah, Englander," he said. He proceeded to blindfold both me and the assistant and then to handcuff us with our hands behind our backs. Into the bell tent we went. He spun it round a few times and we came out still cuffed and blindfolded except that her bra had gone. "Naughty Englander," he said, as I returned to my table blushing furiously. He walked over to the table and removed the bra from the inside pocket of my jacket. Cue enormous applause from my table. How had he done it? Magic, of course. I couldn't have had a better 21st, and it was all thanks to my German colleagues.

There were still shifts to be done at RAF Butzweiler-hof, mainly night ones. Sometimes I would do the night shift and then travel to Cologne to be at BFN during the day, snatching little bits of sleep in one of the bedrooms at Marienburg. Gradually, I was being given more shows at BFN, standing in for people who were away. There was also a system whereby you could buy yourself off an RAF shift. Underpaid airmen were only too happy to pick up an extra ten shillings and I went through the savings I'd made from my writing job by buying myself off so many shifts that I was spending the vast major-ity of my time at BFN. It was, as people say today, a no-brainer. I loved my time at BFN listening to the music of the day and hated my time with the RAF listening to Morse code.

There was great excitement when recording stars came to visit us at BFN. The first one I met was Marion Ryan who came over to sing to the troops. She had just had a hit record, 'Love Me Forever', and was a regular on the TV series, *Spot the Tune*. She was a fine-looking woman – Marilyn Monroe-esque – and the troops loved her. When we had our picture taken with Bill Crozier, then host of *Family Favourites*, I was quick to send it home to my father who posted it to the *Wimbledon Boro News*. They published it together with news of my progress in Germany. Ten years later Marion's twin boys, Paul and Barry, would be pop stars with records in the charts.

Our next visitor was the hottest new pop star, Cliff Richard, who flew out to Cologne to promote his record, 'Livin' Doll'. I got to interview Cliff for my show, *Hey There*, and found him just the nicest guy you could ever meet. I would meet him several times in the future and never change that opinion. It was one of my earliest interviews and also one of the earliest for Cliff. I was 20 and he was 18. Our interview over, I was in the audience when Cliff entertained the troops at Butzweilerhof. He was then a guest in the officers' mess. As an airman, I wasn't allowed in there, but I pushed my luck and broke the rules. Compared with our shabby barracks, it was

With the glamorous Marion Ryan, Germany, 1959

interesting to see how the other half lived. Would anybody recognise me and realise that David Hamilton, the disc-jockey, was also SAC Pilditch? The different name helped, and luckily I got away with it and didn't get marched out.

Sixty years later, I was contacted by a German listener, Axel Reiss, who had recorded the interview off his wireless at his home in Hamburg. He flew over to London and gave it to me. There were the voices of the very young Cliff Richard and the very young David Hamilton. The magic of radio. You never know what might turn up.

The first international star who came to visit us was Connie Francis, who brought with her a copy of her record, 'Lipstick on Your Collar'. She was small, dark-haired and very attractive. She met a dozen of us at the studios and remembered all our names. We were enormously impressed. I learnt later it was something Americans tend to be good at, a form of Pelmanism. When she turned to me and said, "What do you think, David?" I nearly spilled my drink – which, by the way, was lemonade. Here was I, a little sprog in the RAF, and here was this movie and singing star calling me by my name. Naturally, 'Lipstick on Your Collar' got lots of plays on BFN, made it onto *Family Favourites* and became a huge hit. She also agreed to pose with a football with the BFN soccer team and to be our mascot for the day. She wasn't short of offers to lift her onto the piano for a picture in the BFN hallway.

Any work servicemen did on the radio station was voluntary and by buying myself off shifts at Butzweilerhof I was nearly broke. When I had some leave in the summer of '59, Beryl flew out for a week and booked into a hotel in Cologne. She was thrilled that I had

*Connie Francis agrees to be mascot of the
BFN football team, Cologne, 1959*

achieved my ambition to work in radio, and I was able to
do some shows and then spend time with her.

By this time I was spending so little time with the
RAF that I was living in civilian clothes far more than in
uniform. Virtually the only time I went to Butzweilerhof
was to salute and pick up my measly pay packet.

I had become very sloppy and when I turned up for
pay parade with no shoelaces, it was no great surprise
that I was put on a charge. Perhaps I had been spotted
in the officers' mess at the Cliff Richard show, after all,
because when Squadron Leader Satterthwaite told me I
was confined to camp for a week and had to report to
the military police he added with some relish, I thought,
"That means that you won't be able to do your radio
show on Sunday." What he had not reckoned with was
that I had recorded one show in advance, just in case
such an occasion might arise.

The military police were notoriously hard nuts but
when they discovered my links to BFN they were very

lenient with me. "Could you get us messages to home on *Family Favourites*?" they asked. "Of course I can," I said. After that, instead of giving me menial tasks to do, they let me lie on the bed all day and even brought me cups of tea. While I was doing my week's jankers I discovered that Squadron Leader Satterthwaite's first name was Bill. So the following Sunday, with the shoelaces incident very much in mind, I sent him a message on air... "This is for Bill, and I know this is your favourite record." With that I played Dodie Stevens and 'Pink Shoelaces'.

There was no doubt I rebelled against authority. I hated forces life. When National Servicemen were invited to sign on for another year, I wouldn't have signed on for another day. It was the longest two years of my life and I ticked off the days until I could return home, and yet I thanked the RAF for giving me the opportunity to do a job I loved. Could I do it professionally and earn a living from it? Ian Woolf gave me a letter of recommendation, tempered with the line... "Under proper guidance, he could have a good career in broadcasting." What could he mean? Armed with that, I returned to England in time for Christmas 1959, looking forward to a new decade that would be more interesting than I could ever have guessed.

CHAPTER 4

To Manchester and Newcastle

WHAT kept servicemen going was the knowledge that there was someone waiting for them at home when it was all over. What they feared was a 'Dear John'. I got my 'Dear John' shortly before my time in Germany was up. Beryl told me she felt we should end our relationship as she had met someone else. (Later, she told me this wasn't true. She'd made it up because she felt that I would want to end it.) Actually, I wasn't too bothered. I had changed a lot in my two years' service, I was skint and the last thing I wanted was to settle down.

Nonetheless, it was a sad last trip on the train journey to Cuffley that we had done so many times as I went to collect some of my belongings and say goodbye to Beryl and her parents. I insisted she keep our joint record collection. Too many memories there. She was adamant that I shouldn't return to my mother's flat where my bedroom was so damp she thought it was bad for my health. But my father had already told me he didn't want me back. "Delia and I have been very happy while you've been away. You're too old to be living at home." Poor Delia. She must have dreaded the return of the wayward and wilful stepson. I had no money, so how was I going to afford to live somewhere else? But I got the message loud and clear.

Things had changed a lot at ATV, who were forced by law to restore my job on demob. They had moved out of Kingsway to new offices in Marble Arch. When I arrived there, I discovered Harold Jamieson had moved upwards to assistant programme controller and I was now answerable to the Head of Presentation, John Terry. He was smooth and oily and smoked cigarettes in a long cigarette holder. He was pretty awful to me, which I took personally, though looking back I realise he simply didn't want or need another scriptwriter. He already had three – Larry Signy, Gerry Deutsch and Maurice Kaufman, a team that had been assembled while I was away. I was surplus to requirements and a drain on his budget. I had to present all scripts to him for his approval. He would find fault with them and tell me to re-write them. When I complained he said, "If you don't like it, quit." He must have said that half a dozen times.

There were very few openings for DJs in UK radio. The few record shows the BBC Light Programme had were hosted by band leaders like Jack Payne and Jack Jackson or comedians like Sam Costa. I did an audition for Radio Luxembourg at their London studios in Hertford Street. It would have been the perfect job for me – following in the footsteps of my broadcasting hero, Pete Murray, and far from home, where I felt unwelcome. I didn't get the job but, by a quirk of fate, years later the person who turned me down was writing scripts for me so I asked him why. "You sounded pseudo-American," he said. Maybe I was trying too hard but I was attempting to fit in with the station sound.

It wasn't a great year or much of a start to the sixties. I cheered myself up by buying my first car. A colleague in the RAF had said to me, "You must get a car when you get out. It'll give you so much freedom." He was right, of course. I bought a Morris Minor – the Morry Plod – from my stepcousin Robin. It had a split windscreen and those arm trafficators that stuck out left or right when you were turning. I learnt to drive in it and my driving instructor gave me good advice when he suggested I take my test on early closing day when the traffic was lighter. That's what I did in Morden, Surrey, and passed first time. I still remember the number plate: OBP 7. I remembered it from my father's name – Old Bill Pilditch.

Unfortunately, I burnt out the clutch on it when it got stuck in a ditch while a female colleague from ATV and I were enjoying some shenanigans on Wimbledon Common. Well, I couldn't invite her home.

As I was about to write off 1960 as a dead loss, something came up in October that turned everything round. ABC TV was the weekend contractor in the North and Midlands of England, one of the big ITV companies along with ATV and Granada. They were looking for an announcer on a short-term contract at their studios in Manchester. Mel Oxley, one of the announcers, was taking a break to visit his ailing mother in South Africa. No one knew how long that break would be, but it would be likely to cover Christmas and New Year. When I turned up for an audition at the ABC studios at Teddington the Head of Presentation, Geoffrey Lugg, gave me a copy of *TV Times* and asked me to ad-lib to camera for a minute about an evening's programmes. I was told later there were 300 applicants but I had a distinct advantage. With my scriptwriting job I knew all the TV programmes and the phraseology that was used to promote them.

"Val Parnell's *Sunday Night at the London Palladium*, live from the world's greatest variety theatre. The pick of the stars from the pick of the world."

I got the job! So on a Friday night in October 1960, not long after my 22nd birthday I was on a train to Manchester to stay overnight at the El Morocco hotel near the Manchester studios. The following morning I walked down the road to the ABC studios which were in a converted cinema in Didsbury. The downstairs area had been adapted, retaining some seats for audiences for shows like *Opportunity Knocks* with a large stage area. The announcers' studio was upstairs in what in the cinema days had been a broom cupboard. As I soon discovered it was hot and claustrophobic, with a chair, a desk and a locked-on camera very close to the announcer.

On my first day I met John Benson, the senior announcer, who was very welcoming, gave me lots of tips and generally put me at ease. As I watched him in action, I got to admire his style. He had a great voice, later to be heard on *Sale of the Century* – "Tonight from Norwich" – and *The Eamonn Andrews Show*, and oodles of personality.

When it came to my first appearance in the broom cupboard, it was so hot under the bright studio lights that my palms were sweaty, my throat was dry and my heart seemed to be leaping out of my body. I seriously wondered if I had the right temperament for the job. There I was – no autocue, having to remember all the words about the programmes I was promoting, and very much on trial. As I opened the studio door and walked out into the control room, I uttered the words, "Was that alright?" It was a phrase I learned over time not to use because it reeked of insecurity. Not only that, but you'll never get an honest answer.

The one thing nobody had told me was that after 7 p.m., announcers wore dinner jackets and bow ties. It was a throwback to the Reithian principle that it gave everything a sense of occasion. How it went down with viewers in the North and Midlands is hard to say, but thankfully it was a custom that was abandoned in the near future. I had never owned a dinner suit, but John Benson kindly lent me his. Since he was somewhat taller and slimmer than me, there was a vast amount of white shirt where it wouldn't do up and the sleeves were so long I had to keep my hands under the desk. After my first weekend in Manchester, the report came back... David Hamilton did well but looked slightly uncomfortable in a dinner jacket. I'll say.

Mel Oxley's sabbatical drifted on for four months and I was working seven days a week – scriptwriting at ATV Monday to Friday and taking the train to Manchester on Friday evenings, returning to London on the sleeper on Sunday nights. As I'd settled down at ABC and grown in confidence, I was enjoying the job but I knew it couldn't last. In January 1961, another opportunity came along. Tyne-Tees TV were looking for an announcer at their studios in Newcastle-upon-Tyne. Once again there was an audition to be done, with plenty of competition. Denver Thornton, one of their floor managers, travelled to London to see the candidates. Tyne-Tees had an alternative magazine to *TV Times* called *The Viewer*. Denver handed me a copy of that and once again I was asked to ad lib to camera for a minute. I pulled out of my pocket the stopwatch I used at ATV to time scripts and spoke for exactly 60 seconds. Denver later joked that it was the stopwatch that got me the job. I signed a contract to go to Newcastle for a year.

This was going to make several people happy. My father and Delia would no longer have me under their feet and John Terry would no longer have a surplus scriptwriter. After his many offers that I should quit, I walked into his office and said, "I quit."

"Have you got another job?" he asked, blinking heavily.

"I've got two," I said with some feeling of joy. The same as the number of fingers I'd like to have offered him.

By February 1961, I was no longer a writer but about to become a full-time broadcaster. To celebrate my new career I bought myself a new car – a Riley 1.5 – and headed in it up the long and winding road to Newcastle.

It so happened that my old colleague from CFN, John Dightam, was working at Tyne-Tees as a Transmission Controller and he invited me to stay with him and his wife at Monkseaton until I could find digs. The announcing team was Adrian Cairns, an ex-actor who was Chief announcer; John Kelley, a tall and handsome man who married the daughter of the Programme Controller, Bill Lyon Shaw; and Valerie Dennis. On my first night on air I watched a programme called *Tyne-Tees Personality of the Year*. It was a variety show and at the end there were three awards – male and female personalities and producer of the year. I vowed there and then that the following year it was going to be me receiving the male award. How was I going to do it when I was up against singers, comedians and other established presenters? I didn't know, but that was my aim.

Tyne-Tees covered a big chunk of the North East of England, Tyneside, Wearside and Teesside. As the Wear was the third big river in between the Tyne and the Tees, the locals felt it should be called Tyne, Wear and Tees Television, and that might have been the case had bosses not noticed that the initials would spell TWAT Television. The station's bosses were George and Alfred Black, seasoned impresarios and one-time owners of the London Palladium, and they had built a station that was so popular that autograph hunters were often to be seen on the steps outside. There were plenty of stars for them to see because there was a daily variety show at lunchtime, *The One O'Clock Show*, with resident comedians and singers. With their showbiz contacts the Blacks were able to lure the biggest stars to Tyneside. There was great excitement when Shirley Bassey travelled North to sing with the Tyne-Tees band.

As well as the lunchtime variety show, TTT provided Geordies with local news and had sports, quiz and pop programmes as well as children's shows. By the early sixties, most people had a television set and, unlike the multi-channels today, there were only two, BBC and ITV, so audiences were huge. For someone like me, starting out in television, Tyne-Tees provided the perfect training ground. As part of my contract I appeared as an announcer, read local news and occasionally hosted shows.

After a month with the Dightams, I found some digs with a lovely landlady called Mrs Hall just around the corner from the Spanish City in Whitley Bay. I'd always

In Tyne-Tees TV studio with Judith Chalmers

fancied living by the seaside, but the North East coast was so bracing I don't think I went in the sea once. When my mother came up to stay in a hotel at Christmas time she said she'd never been so cold in her life.

If the weather was cold, the people were warm and took us to their hearts even if we were soft Southerners. After a while on screen I started getting invited to events. One of my first invitations was to referee a charity football match in the mining town of Stanley. After the match the hospitality was pretty generous and when I got back to Tyne-Tees to read the evening news I realised I'd had far too much to drink. I put my head under the tap in the loo to try frantically to sober up and when it came to the bulletin I was digging my nails into my hands to help me get my act together. I learnt a lesson from that and from then on vowed I would never, ever drink before I worked. It's been my golden rule ever since.

I found a good pal in Bill Steel, one of the transmission controllers at TTT. Bill – inspired by me, I like to think – went on to be an announcer, hosted the evening news programme at TTT and even appeared as an actor in *Coronation Street*. In 1961 he helped me find the entertainment spots in Newcastle, we met some nice ladies and had some good laughs. One night we did a pub crawl from Tynemouth to Whitley Bay, a distance of two and a half miles. We set out to drink a pint in every pub on the way. We swear we did it, though I doubt if we remember how many pubs it was. Luckily, no newsreading that night!

Early in my time at Tyne-Tees I met a girl called Hilary who was a weather presenter on the station. We started seeing each other and got on well together. So much so that my father and Delia travelled up and met her and her parents in the lovely town of Kendal. I think both families hoped this might be the real thing. Sadly, before long Hilary left Tyne-Tees – I know not why – and moved away from the area.

I later dated a vision mixer from the station who was a peroxide blonde. We went for dinner at the County Hotel, next door to the railway station. The waiter, who was very camp, asked me what I would like to drink. I told him whisky and dry, which was my tipple at the time. He looked at my companion and said, "And for Madam – brown ale?" She was livid. "Why did he think I would drink brown ale?" I didn't have an answer for that but it was about the rudest thing I'd ever heard.

There was a booker at Tyne-Tees called Myrna Malinsky. She called me into her office one day and said a new club was opening at Low Fell called The Lido. They were booking cabaret acts and were looking for a compere to introduce them on three nights a week, and she had recommended me. The pay was a fiver a night, which would nicely supplement my Tyne-Tees wages of £30 a week. The announcing schedule took up two afternoons and two evenings a week so mostly I was able to arrange to have evenings off to do the Lido gig. One night, when I was double-booked, I found a way round it. There was an *Armchair Theatre* production that ran 90 minutes. I introduced it, leapt into the car and drove across the Tyne bridge to Low Fell, changed into dinner suit, introduced the great comedian Dick Emery on stage, changed and raced back to the TV studio in time to introduce the next programme. Strictly speaking, I should have been there all the time in case of a breakdown, but I got away with it. Another act I introduced at the Lido was The Springfields, who included Dusty Springfield and her brother Tom and who a year later would have a hit with 'Island of Dreams'. Dusty was just 22 but it was obvious she would go on to become a huge star, in my opinion our greatest female singer ever.

I was the same age as Dusty and there was a rest-lessness in me. I was always curious to know what was round the corner. With that in mind, I set off one day in the Riley 1.5 up the coast road from Whitley Bay to visit the fine city of Edinburgh. My first visit to Scotland was a disaster. Suddenly, for no reason I can recall, the car was upside-down in a field near Dunbar with a Matt Monro record blaring out of the radio. Fortunately, it wasn't 'Softly as I Leave You'. Was there an adverse camber in the road or was it a case of a young, inexpe-rienced driver? Probably the latter. I was a bit battered and bruised but determined to make it to Edinburgh, so I gathered up some contents in a box in the boot of the car, including some muddy football boots which I must have needed in a few days, and caught a bus that would take me there. I rocked up to the Caledonian Hotel where I was viewed with suspicion by the commissionaire. Not surprising. I looked like I had been in a street fight.

"I'd like a room, please," I said shakily.

"That'll be £3-17-6," he said. "But we'll need a wee deposit."

"How much?"

"£3-17-6."

When I got to my room and looked in the mirror I can see why he thought I looked dodgy.

A couple of days later I was back on screen. By now the early nerves had gone. I was really enjoying the job and putting more personality into it. The word announcer was very formal. I liked to think of ourselves more as programme hosts, a friendly face coming into your home and sharing the viewing with you. In the afternoons there was quite a lot of time to fill between programmes, so I introduced a glove puppet called Tobee – so named because it didn't know if it was going Tobee a boy or a girl. Jack Saltman, one of the scriptwriters, was the voice of Tobee and operated him while crouching behind the desk. We bounced off each other and enjoyed a jocular repartee. The kids loved Tobee.

Sometimes in the evening I would dress up. Introducing *Emergency Ward 10*, I'd wear a white coat and point a stethoscope at the camera. "Hello, Doctor Hamilton here. You're not looking too good this evening. I recommend a nice lie down in *Emergency Ward 10*." Or introducing a western, I'd come on in a Stetson. "Howdy partners, it's time to mosey on down to the OK Corral."

Somehow it worked, and early in 1962 when all the votes were counted I was nominated Tyne-Tees TV Male Personality Of The Year. Vera Lynn travelled to

Vera Lynn presents Personality of the Year awards at Tyne-Tees Television, 1962

Newcastle to present the trophies in a big variety show to Female Personality, singer Shirley Weston, Producer of the Year Keith Beckett and me.

Having achieved my goal, I decided to move on. I was grateful to Tyne-Tees for all the opportunities they had given me but it was time to swim in a bigger pond.

CHAPTER 5

Manchester in the Sixties

I
T was Southern TV in Southampton who came calling with the offer of a year's contract as announcer/ newsreader early in 1962. No audition needed this time as I had previous form. When I arrived at the studios in Northam, on the banks of the River Itchen, I met a Head of News who had what I thought at the time was a crackpot idea. He had his newsreaders standing up at a lectern, rather like a vicar in a pulpit. When I asked him why, he said their jackets hung better and they projected more. Ironically, lots of newsreaders stand up these days (without the lectern), so maybe he was a man ahead of his time.

Not long after I started in Southampton, ABC came back to me and said Mel Oxley had left and they now had a full-time vacancy in Manchester. ABC was a much bigger company than Southern and had much more power on the ITV network. For the only time in my career I broke a contract and told Southern I was taking the ABC job. They took it badly. I offered to carry on doing three days a week until they found a replacement but could only do weekdays as I would be on at weekends at ABC. This didn't go down well with the other announcers who valued their weekends off. Southern paid me very poorly – just 12 guineas for three days' work – but they also gave me expenses for my hotel accommodation. By not staying in a hotel on the third night I could make a little more. One of the other announcers was Richard Davies, later re-named the more friendly Dickie Davies by Jimmy Hill. Our voices were so similar that Southern wouldn't let us read voice-overs on local commercials on each other's shifts. I lasted four months at Southern. They never used me again. No more than I deserved.

Having been born in Manchester, I felt that something was drawing me back there. When I got back again to ABC, my eye fell on an attractive, dark-haired girl who worked in the make-up department. Her name was Sheila Moore, and I found myself hoping that she would be doing my make-up before I went on screen. Finally, I plucked up courage to invite her out and discovered she was seeing someone else who worked in outside broadcasts. It was then that I took a leaf out of Bill Pilditch's book and eliminated the competition. She was living with her parents in their off licence in Sale but I invited her to move in with me to a flat I had started renting in Palatine Road, Didsbury, not far from the studios.

Being based in the North was good because Tyne-Tees invited me back to host a series called *Cue For Sport*. With football being like a religion in the North East there was much interest in the big clubs, Newcastle, Sunderland and Middlesbrough, as well as local speedway, cricket and golf. My run on *Cue For Sport* lasted only three months before I was replaced by the announcer who succeeded me and did the programme as part of his contract – i.e. cost the company nothing. Hard lesson learnt early on. No matter how well you do something, you can't compete with someone who does it free. In fairness, my successor Mike Neville was a local boy who probably knew a lot more about sport and the area than I did and went on to become a Geordie legend. And in fairness to Tyne-Tees, they came up with more series for me to host over the next few years.

One weekend, for a change, ABC asked me to do my announcing stint from their studio in Aston, Birmingham. While there I called Sheila who gave me the bombshell news that she was pregnant. Inevitable, I suppose. We were having far too much fun for our own good. "Then we must get married," I said. It was the decent thing that people did in those days but when I thought about it, I felt that was what I wanted to do anyway. A register office wedding was hastily arranged and the chosen date was Guy Fawkes' Day. John Benson was due to be the best man but was working in London so Dougie Fairbairn, one of the transmission controllers, deputised. Sheila and I giggled our way through most of the ceremony. For our honeymoon we stayed at the Hotel Du Mont Blanc, a charming old fashioned hotel with a creaky lift in the Latin Quarter of Paris, a short walk from Notre Dame cathedral. We spent our time sightseeing, walking along the banks of the Seine and enjoying the sights of Paris. Before the week was over we ran out of money and lived on bags of chips.

Hardly was the trip over before I had to drive to Newcastle to record commercials for *The Viewer*, the magazine that had given me my trophy as Tyne-Tees Male Personality of the Year.

Drives across the Pennines would become more frequent as Tyne-Tees offered me more shows. With a baby on the way and three mouths to feed I was going to have to do a lot more than just my weekend announcing job at ABC, especially as we had bought our first house, a bungalow in Marple near Stockport.

In December 1962, I did my first radio broadcast in the UK. Geoff Lawrence, one of the BBC producers based in Manchester, invited me to stand in for Gay Byrne, the regular host of *The Beat Show* which was recorded on Monday nights in front of an audience at the Playhouse Theatre in Hulme and transmitted on the BBC Light Programme the following Thursday lunchtime. The show featured the BBC Northern Dance Orchestra with guest appearances from singers and groups of the beat music era, often Manchester bands like Wayne Fontana and the Mindbenders or Liverpool bands like The Searchers or Swinging Blue Jeans. The teenage audience loved the beat groups and tolerated the orchestra with a rather bored air. I opened the show with Gay Byrne's usual intro... "It's *The Beat Show* with Bernard Herrmann and the NDO, the band with the beat's that reet." In reality, it wasn't that reet but typical BBC compromise and the best they could do back then. In time Gay Byrne would be off more and I'd stand in, becoming the regular host by 1965. It led to my hosting more radio shows for the BBC in the North of England – variety shows like *Mid-day Music Hall* and *On Stage-Scarborough*, and eventually shows for the Beeb in London. Though Manchester had two thriving ITV stations, Granada and ABC, London was still the place to be in the sixties, the broadcasting hub.

Another job that came up one night a week was playing records for the skaters at the Silver Blades Ice Rink in Manchester. I was getting more and more involved in music which suited me fine, as I was such a fan.

In March 1963, ABC asked me to interview a new group called The Beatles on their Saturday night show, *ABC at Large*. There was a great buzz about The Beatles, who had had two hit records, 'Love Me Do' and 'Please Please Me'. On March 2 they dashed from a performance in Sheffield on the *Helen Shapiro Show* to the

Didsbury studios where I interviewed them live, along with their manager Brian Epstein and his latest protegé Gerry Marsden, of Gerry and the Pacemakers. Brian was very charming and professional; Gerry, the enthusiastic youngster, eager to please. The Beatles were more difficult – four people who knew each other well, were aware of their impending destiny and not much bothered about playing along with a green 24-year-old interviewer. John Lennon had a prickly wit and I think regarded me as a posh Southerner. It was one of their first TV interviews. No tape of it remains so it's impossible to judge it. A month later, The Beatles had their first Number 1. Apparently, the interview went well enough as I was invited to introduce them on stage at the Urmston Show in Abbotsfield Park, Manchester, the following August Bank Holiday Monday. The show was done in a huge marquee with a number of supporting acts including Brian Poole and the Tremeloes. When I introduced The Beatles the audience of teenage girls stampeded the stage and I thought the marquee was going to collapse. I leapt off the stage to safety and listened to them in the park. Tickets to see The Beatles were ten shillings and my fee was £10. It was A Hard Day's Night.

Just two months before the Urmston Show I had become a father. It was a nervous young man who turned up at Ashton-upon-Mersey maternity hospital on 7 June 1963. There was no question of husbands being present at the birth in those days. Instead it was a nerve-wracking pacing up and down in the corridors. I suppose, being an only son of an only son, I was hoping for a boy. When I discovered Sheila had had a girl, I was delighted, relieved that mother and daughter were both fine. We called her Jane. She would grow into a beautiful young woman.

In November 1963, Sheila got a call she could have

done without – a knock on the door in the middle of the night from a policeman telling her that her husband was in Leeds Infirmary, following a bad car crash. She rushed Jane round to her parents' home and drove across country to Leeds. There she found me looking bruised and battered with 26 stitches in my face. I had replaced the Riley 1.5, which I wrote off, with an MGB sports car. I drove back in it at night after a stint at Tyne-Tees. (Due on air at ABC the next day.) In those days before the M26 Trans Pennine motorway the drive from Newcastle to Manchester was never an easy one. On this particular night I ran into thick fog. In Garforth, near Leeds, the cats' eyes ran out and, not being able to see the Halt sign, I drove straight across the main Leeds to Hull trunk road, into an eight-foot drop and landed in a beck. Thank goodness nothing was coming along the trunk road or I'd have been killed for sure. As it was, my ribs were crushed by the steering wheel and as my head hit the sun roof the clip sliced open my nose and my right eyelid. The horn jammed and luckily the people who ran the pub near the T-junction heard the noise, got me out of the car and into the pub and rang the police. I was such a mess that an agent who came to see me in hospital said, "With a face like that you've got a great future in radio." A thought I kept in mind for the future. I didn't work for a month, and over New Year 1964, Sheila and I took a trip to the Canaries to let the sunshine heal some of the scars. On the trip Sheila, never a happy flyer, found a use for the sick bag on the plane and discovered she was pregnant again. The following August our son was born. Because we couldn't think of any other names we liked we called him David. He would grow up to be a fine young man, a journalist, like his grandfather.

How clever of my wife to have given me a girl and a

boy, one of each. Along with our dog, Lulu, we were a cosy unit at our bungalow in Marple. For the first time in my life I had a home where I felt welcome and a proper family life. I had a lovely rapport with the audiences who watched ABC at the weekend. Lots of people wrote nice letters and a lady called Grace Bolton, who lived in Salford, baked a cake and sent it to me at every birthday and Christmas. Some people sent things for the babies when they heard about them.

On Sunday nights ABC had a blockbuster schedule that everyone watched. *Armchair Theatre*, with top British actors; *Sunday Night at the London Palladium*, live variety with big stars from around the world: *Maverick*, the western; and *The Avengers*, the cult series with Patrick Macnee and lovely co-stars like Diana Rigg and Honor Blackman. Everyone went to work on Monday morning talking about the same programmes they had seen the night before, something that wouldn't happen today. One Sunday night, Shirley Bassey decided not to sing one of her songs and the Palladium show under-ran by four minutes. As he rolled into the commercial break, the transmission controller told me, "Get into the studio. You've got four minutes to fill." Four minutes, with only the *TV Times* to tell me about the rest of the programmes for that night and some Granada ones – of which I knew very little – for the next day. I earned my money that night. When you've done that, any other TV presenting comes easy. With only two channels anyone appearing on television became a celebrity, even announcers, and I started getting lots of requests to open fêtes and carnivals.

One day a letter arrived at the Didsbury studios from an agent, Carl Gresham, based in Bradford. The letterhead showed a large picture of him in a dodgy white raincoat, a bit like the 'Man in the Strand' cigarettes ad

– 'You're never alone with a strand'. Carl had worked as an extra on *Coronation Street*, where he became friendly with the likes of Pat Phoenix and Bill Roache and discovered that when not acting in The Street they enjoyed pressing the flesh of the viewers, signing autographs and receiving nice brown envelopes in return.

"Any requests you get, pass on to me and I'll deal with them. And I'll get you more," said Carl. In no time he had me dashing around to events in the North of England, often accompanied by the *TV Times* mascot, Tivvy, a gonk the kids loved. I loved meeting the viewers but also discovering the industrial towns and cities of the North which were still re-building after the war. It was an interesting time in Northern England, where the Mersey sound and, to an extent, the Manchester sound were plundering the music charts and where so many kitchen sink films were set – like *Room at the Top*, *A Taste of Honey*, *A Kind of Loving* and *This Sporting Life*. Sheila and I loved watching them at the cinema and then I loved seeing the places where they were filmed while on my travels. I was always interested to know what was round the corner.

By 1964 another band had come along to rival The Beatles, The Rolling Stones, and I was invited to introduce them on stage at the Palace Theatre, Manchester. Pop concerts were done like variety shows, with several acts appearing before the top of the bill. The audiences were mainly teenage girls and had little interest in the support acts. My every appearance was greeted by cries of "We want the Stones," not very encouraging for the next act waiting in the wings, especially for girl singers like Julie Grant who'd had a couple of chart hits. Tough for the compere as well. No room for comedy. I remember asking one comedian who hosted lots of pop shows how he handled it. "I told them I was going to stand on my head until they shut up. So I did that for about two minutes and they started applauding. It filled up my slot and I got off to applause." I should have learnt to stand on my head. There was a nasty surprise when the show was over. I had parked my MGB car (put back together after the crash) at the back of the theatre. Somebody thought it was Mick Jagger's car and scratched a love note on it. For a week I drove round with I LOVE YOU MICK on the bonnet of my car. The re-spray cost me more than my fee for the show.

I seem to have been unlucky with cars. After the MGB I bought a green Aston Martin. When Sheila saw it her face dropped. "Green is an unlucky colour," she said. I scoffed at the superstition. On my next trip to Newcastle I parked it in a side street next to the Tyne-Tees studios.

Outside my first house with Tivvy, the TV
Times mascot, on the green Aston Martin

While we were recording, one of the technicians said to me, "Is that your Aston Martin in the side street? All the side of it has been ripped in." I thought he was kidding – the sort of joke technicians play on performers in the studio. When I left, I realised it was no joke. It appeared that a lorry with an overhanging load had ripped in the entire length of one side of the car. It was almost impossible to open the door and get into it. It was a very sheepish DH who drove into the home driveway in Marple. Never again would I buy a green car.

Working every weekend with ABC was an odd existence. I was working when most people were off. When I had time off, nearly everyone was at work. Sheila spent her weekends happily with the kids or her parents. Once a week we'd have a meal out at Stanneyland's Steak House in Stockport with a typical '60s menu – prawn cocktail, Steak Diane, flambéd at your table and a pudding that was Crêpes Suzette or Baked Alaska, accompanied by that sweet white wine we drank in the sixties like Niersteiner or Liebfraumilch, and rounded off with an Irish whiskey. We wouldn't touch wine like that today. Ugh! Sheila, in fact, is now teetotal and vegetarian. How we change through our lifetimes.

Living in the Manchester area I got to know some of the cast of *Coronation Street* – among them Jennifer Moss, who played Lucille Hewitt. My stepcousin Robin, who was selling jewellery, was staying with us for a couple of days and Jennifer offered to take us to a club near the Grand Union Canal called the Garden of Eden. She warned me in advance, "Everyone you think is a man is a woman and everyone you think is a woman is a man." After a while we got talking to a couple, Paul and Josie, obviously really Joe. She was tall and dark, fine-looking. Only the large Adam's apple might have been a giveaway. Not to Robin, who was rather taken with her. "It's a man," I whispered in his ear. As the drinks flowed Josie started talking about her clients. It became clear that she was on the game and her speciality was oral sex in cars. "What happens if you get a hand up the skirt?" I asked. Josie pulled herself up to her full height and her voice deepened. "In that case I'm a bleedin' great bloke, ain't I?" We didn't stay long after that. Robin headed back South a little older and wiser.

Occasionally in Manchester I would meet some of the footballers from that fine city, knocking down a pile of coins that had been raised in a pub for charity with the wonderful Bobby Charlton and playing in a team, the Northern TV Stars, that I formed with Freddie Pye, formerly on the books of Man U and later a director at Man City.

A cold day in Manchester with Kenny Lynch and stars of Coronation Street

I also met Abe Sacks who called himself 'Tailor to the Stars'. He often advertised in the *Manchester Evening News* with pictures of him with Herman's Hermits, who were among his star clients. I went to see him to make suits for me that I could wear on television and he signed me up as his latest star. I became very friendly with Abe and his son Michael and he invited me along to boxing nights where wealthy men in dinner jackets and bow ties would have dinner and then watch impoverished but ambitious young men in a ring knocking eight bells out of each other. I couldn't do it now.

Abe was also a racehorse owner and took me to Wolverhampton to see one of his horses run. At 7-1 it looked like a good bet. I was about to put a few quid on it when Percy Allden, the trainer, tugged my sleeve. "We're not trying today," he said. As I saw people putting money on it, I felt like saying, "Not trying today," but I wasn't quite that stupid. Next time out the horse won at 25-1. This time, one assumes, it was trying.

Away from Manchester, there were more trips to Newcastle, which must have been worrying for Sheila

With Eric Burdon from The Animals. Tyne-Tees TV Rehearsal Room, 1964

with the difficult cross-country road trip. Tyne-Tees came up with a pop music series for me to host. *Rehearsal Room* featured local beat groups, the biggest of which was The Animals who'd recently had a huge international hit with 'The House of the Rising Sun'. This led to me co-hosting *It's the Geordie Beat* at the City Hall, Newcastle with Alan Freeman. Fluff Freeman was one of the big DJs at the time and the producer suggested I pick him up from Newcastle airport. When his plane landed all the passengers disembarked and there was no sight of Fluff. *Had he missed the flight?* I wondered. I waited for about ten minutes and was about to leave when suddenly there he was, walking down the steps with his suit cover draped over his arm. It turned out he had been mobbed by the crew who all wanted his autograph. Such was the power of DJs at the time. I knew that was where I wanted to be.

Tyne-Tees followed up with more series for me to do; *Singalong*, a pop series co-hosted with the singer Millie who'd had a big hit with 'My Boy Lollipop'; *The Bright Sparks*, a quiz series for kids; and *Pop the Question*,

With Millie on Singalong, *Tyne-Tees TV, 1967*

77

another quiz show – series 1 co-hosted with Judith Chalmers and series 2 with Sheila Tracey. All those ladies were an absolute joy to work with.

Another thriving ITV station was Anglia TV. Based in Norwich, they produced *Waggoner's Walk*, one of the first TV soaps; *Survival*, the wonderful wildlife series; *Tales of the Unexpected*, great drama; *Day By Day*, a daily magazine show, local farming programmes and local football including the hotly contested derby match between Norwich and Ipswich. Another difficult cross-country journey – Manchester to Norwich – but I went there regularly as a relief announcer, standing in for other announcers who were away. While there I let the programme controller know that, although I was happy to do the announcing work, what I really wanted to do was programme hosting. In time they would come up with something that would change my life.

Back home I had the wonderful stability of married life and watching my delightful children growing up, but something was still gnawing away at me, that one-eyed monster – ambition. The need to be known on a national scale. I auditioned for two jobs I didn't get. Eamonn Andrews was leaving *World of Sport* and ABC were looking for a replacement. I was on a shortlist of three and went to Teddington for the audition. The job went to my old colleague Dickie Davies. He had worked before with John Bromley, the Head of Sport, so why would Bromley not choose someone he knew and was sure he could trust? Dickie went to become an immaculate host of the show and was the right man for the job. In hindsight, would I have wanted to be typecast on sport when I was more interested in music? I think not.

The other job I went for was as a newscaster at ITN. Again I didn't get taken on. No reason given. A mispronunciation of Buenos Aires perhaps? All that mucking about in geography lessons now taking its toll.

Among all the lovely letters I was receiving at ABC, some nasty ones were beginning to arrive. After a while I started recognising the addresses and chucked them in the bin without reading them. Then the letter writer started sending them to my bosses. One day I got a call from one of the exec's saying, "We're getting a lot of letters from people saying your appearance is upsetting them. One says seeing you on the screen is making his mother feel ill. I think perhaps we should give you a rest for a while."

"Can I defend myself?" I asked. "All these letters are coming from one person."

"I don't think so," he said. "The handwriting is different and there are lots of different addresses."

"He may be a master of disguising handwriting," I said, fighting to avoid the sack. "I've been getting these letters for some time and I can tell you they all have the same characteristics. The writer always puts his name above the address in the top right corner. Look at other letters, hardly anyone does that. Only one address has a house number. The others have just a street name, no number. Finally, all the addresses are within a 10-mile radius of Doncaster."

He had to admit I was right. I kept my job. Lucky I wasn't let go with no explanation.

CHAPTER 6

To Knotty Ash

THERE had been many false dawns at ABC, things that promised more than they fulfilled, and turned out to be a voice-over at the top of the show or a fleeting appearance. So I had no great expectations when I was booked to do a pilot for a show called *Doddy's Music Box* between Christmas and New Year 1966. All I knew was that Ken Dodd, the star of the show, was huge box office at the time. He'd been Variety Club Entertainer of the Year, had topped the charts with his record, 'Tears', and had had a long-running, sell-out season at the London Palladium. Now ABC had signed him up for their peak time Saturday night show for the ITV network.

As Peter Frazer-Jones, the producer, explained when I arrived at the Didsbury studios, the premise of *Doddy's Music Box* was that Ken Dodd would be the star in the show that would feature songs from many of the pop stars of the day – people like Dusty Springfield, Matt Monro, Tom Jones and Billy Fury – interspersed with sketches featuring Ken and a repertory of actors. ABC were looking for an interviewer for the sketches as David Mahlowe, who he had worked with before, was unavailable since he was under contract to the BBC. It was Ken's idea to use me. "What about that young chap who introduces the programmes?" he said.

The first time we met was on the set at Didsbury

when we were handed our scripts, written by Ken and Eddie Braben. "What do you think, Diddy David?" he said with an obvious reference to his famous diddy men. The audience, which consisted of make up girls, props boys and cameramen suppressed giggles at hearing their announcer being debunked in this way. In fairness to Ken, he took me to one side after rehearsals and said, "Do you mind me calling you that? If so, I won't do it anymore. If not, I think it will stick." I said I didn't mind and I've been stuck with it now for well over fifty years.

My new nickname probably cemented my chances of getting the part and on the first week of January 1967, we launched into what would turn out to be a 10-week series that occupied a Top 10 slot in the ITV ratings. Our working schedule was … rehearsal with scripts on Tuesday; learn the lines at home that night; rehearsal without scripts on Wednesday; record with an audience on Thursday evening. Rehearsals were constantly interrupted by phone calls from Ken's agent, his publicist and even his tailor. *So this is the life of a big star*, I thought, very impressed. Where the sketches were concerned, Ken liked to record twice as much as there was time for. After the recordings he would go into the control room with Peter Frazer-Jones and decide which ones worked best and would appear on the show. The others ended up on the cutting room floor. Actors who travelled up from London to appear on the show – like Graham Stark, John Laurie, Patricia Hayes and Arthur Mullard – never knew if their work would be used or not. I knew that as the interviewer I would always be in some of the sketches, if not all. After a few weeks the cockney actress Rita Webb, who had become a regular, complained to Ken during rehearsals, "'Ere, Ken. All I am on this show is a little fat cow. I'm an actress. Give me some decent lines."

The next week Eddie Braben arrived with the scripts that included a two-hander between Ken and Rita and a solo sketch with Rita as a cockney newsreader, "Right, 'ere's your bleedin' *News at Ten*." Both sketches went well and the audience loved them. For the finale we all walked on, Ken gave us a halfpenny for our fee and our names came up on the screen. We all then had two days wondering if our best bits were left in or cut out.

I would watch the show from my announcer's studio upstairs after linking into it, "Right, off to Studio 1 to join Ken Dodd and the mayhem on *Doddy's Music Box*." Knowing the background to Rita's protestations,

With Doddy and Tivvy

there was added interest on this night to see what of hers would be in the show. I soon found out. Nothing, no double hander, no *News at Ten*. All she did was walk on at the end and get her halfpenny. All the actors were booked a week at a time. When the phone rang on Monday, Rita had the choice to tell them where to stick it or to swallow her pride. She was there on Tuesday and there was no more talk of just being a little fat cow. It sent out a message to everyone. It's the star of the show that calls all the shots. A lesson I learned early on.

The chemistry between Ken and me seemed to work well and, as the series progressed, he started getting requests on his personal appearances to bring Diddy David along as well. For the first one, a supermarket in Liverpool, he suggested I meet him at his home in Knotty Ash. When I arrived there someone showed me into what looked like a waiting room with tickling sticks, Diddy men and gold discs. When Ken came downstairs it was 11 o'clock, the time we were due to open the store, "Come on, I'll show you around," he said. I protested that 11 o'clock was the time we were due to do the opening ceremony. "Don't worry about that," he said. "A crowd will get a bigger crowd." He showed me into three different rooms and in each one pointed at a suite of furniture. "Lewis's, Liverpool," he said in the first one. Then, "Paulden's, Sheffield" and finally, "Lewis's, Manchester." I realised they were suites of furniture he got for making appearances in the stores. "Listen and learn," he said.

When we got to the venue, sure enough the crowd had swollen. Although Ken was a local man and people could see him in the area at any time, they loved to turn up for anything he did – a real local hero who never left Merseyside, unlike Cilla Black and The Beatles. We stayed signing autographs for an hour, until the last person had left. Ken had time for everyone. A bit of patter, "OK, whack? All right, Commander?" When the crowd started to thin out, Ken said to the manager, "Give us a bit of meat for me dinner." "Help yourself, Ken," said the manager, opening the fridge. Ken's fiancée Anita had a huge grip into which went steaks, pork chops, lamb chops, sausages, enough to feed an army. "Listen and learn," he said again, over his shoulder, as we headed for the car. What I learned most was his rapport with the public. It was like a love affair. They loved him and he loved them. Everyone who met him had a slice of Ken Dodd and would never forget him. I'm sure that was one reason they bought his records and went to his shows, why he had such a loyal following and his career lasted so long. If I listened to and learned one thing from Ken, it was how to be with the public. He was a great influence.

More PAs, as we called them, came along. When we opened a supermarket in Oldham, the local *Evening Chronicle* reckoned there was a crowd outside of over 5,000, bringing traffic to a standstill.

My mother had never been a great Ken Dodd fan but when she travelled up from Fulham to stay with us in Marple for a few days, she came along to one of the recordings. She met Ken after the show, and he charmed her. "I can see where he got his good looks from," he said. Another one won over.

While we were recording *Doddy's Music Box* my father was taken ill. I hadn't seen much of him because we lived over 200 miles apart, but he said he hadn't been feeling right for a while and was taken into St Helier Hospital for some tests. Delia and I were called to see a doctor who told us he had lung cancer and had three months to live. My father was a chain-smoker, going through about

60 a day. He carried a cigarette case in his breast pocket with his initials CJP on it. It had a dent in it where it had been hit by a bullet during the war. He said the cigarette case had saved his life. Now its contents were going to kill him. It was impressed on us that we should not tell him. No one could accept the news that they were terminally ill. That's how it was back in 1967. So we lived a lie, constantly telling him that he was getting better while knowing he was going to die. It was heartbreaking, watching him lose more and more weight.

Eventually they let him come home with a day nurse coming to visit him. She was Irish and I didn't think very sympathetic to him so, in the hope of getting to her to warm to him, I mentioned he was born in Dublin.

"Is that right, you're Irish?" she asked him when they were alone together. My father confirmed. "Then you must be a Catholic," she said.

"Lapsed," said my father.

"Once a Catholic, always a Catholic," said the nurse. In his last days, encouraged by her, he went back to Catholicism and on the day he passed away the priest came to the flat to administer the last rights.

In the weeks before he died I tried to get down to London to see him when I could. My mother was staying with us at Marple over Easter and the news of his passing came through on Easter Monday morning. On the train back to London she said, "I should never have left him. He was a good man." *A bit late for that*, I thought.

My father had three watering holes he visited in Wimbledon – the Prince of Wales, the South Western opposite the railway station and The Alexandra. He went between them as he pleased. On the day of his funeral not one person he spent time with in those pubs was there. All those hours spent there, and nobody came to his funeral. What wasted time when he could have been at home with his wife and son.

What, I wondered, had turned him to a life dominated by drink? Was it the horrors of war or had he been like it before? I will never know. Certainly the war changed his life dramatically. Everything that seemed so promising before it turned out to be so difficult afterwards. He was a very bright man and, in between the boozing, gave me some good advice. When I kept my Sam Bartram scrapbooks he said to me, "Don't be a fan of someone else. Be a fan of yourself." He also told me when I was a teenager, "Why try to be like everyone else? You're not. You're different." I wasn't sure how to take that because I wanted to be like everyone else. He was right to tell me to take the messenger boy job at ATV, and right to tell me I was too old to be living at home when I came back from the RAF. It seemed tough at the time but it made me independent, determined to move away and make something of my life.

Because he was such a larger-than-life character I couldn't believe he was gone. A couple of times I walked into The Cock tavern, where he used to start his Fleet Street pub crawl, convinced I would see him there. How could he not be propping up the bar? Could he really be gone at 57?

The only way I could try to get over the loss of him was to throw myself into my work. BBC radio were starting to use me on music shows in London like *Swingalong* and *Swing into Summer* (well, it was the Swinging Sixties); *Newly Pressed* (new releases) and *Music through Midnight*. There were done from the basement studios at Broadcasting House and transmitted on the BBC Light Programme. Apart from *Newly Pressed*, none were all-record shows. Through an agreement with the

Musicians Union, the BBC guaranteed to hire and pay musicians to play for them. Based in all parts of the UK were house orchestras whose members were actually on the BBC staff. Light Programme shows were a mixture of records and sessions recorded at Beeb studios by different bands and singers. When most people wanted to hear the latest chart records, this format was by no means ideal. Presenters still had to write a script that would be approved by the producer. While all this was happening, along came the pirate radio stations that were giving listeners precisely what they wanted – all records and disc jockeys having ad lib fun. I did a 13-week stint on a show called *Mid-day Spin* which, in retrospect, was a try-out for plans the BBC might have in the future.

On Sunday 4 June 1967, the peace was disturbed at our Marple home by a phone call from Dougie Fairbairn at the Didsbury studios. "Get yourself down to the centre of Stockport right away. A plane has come down in the middle of the town and we need to get reports into ITN." Dougie was a well known joker.

"OK, so you want a game of tennis," I said. (Something we often did on Sunday mornings before the day's shifts.)

"I'm serious, mate. Put on a black suit and a black tie right away and get yourself down there ASAP."

It wasn't hard to find where the accident had happened. I followed the billowing smoke and the smell of burning. Not only that, but the huge crowd that had gathered – later estimated at 10,000 – to witness the mayhem of what turned out to be one of the biggest disasters in British aviation history. A British Midland Argonaut carrying holidaymakers home from Mallorca had got into trouble on its way to Ringway airport in Manchester. As it lost height over Stockport, the pilot put it down on the only grassy area near the centre of the town. Miraculously, no one was killed on the ground, but 72 people on the plane lost their lives. Heroic local people risked their lives by carrying passengers out of the burning wreckage to safety. Others came to gawp at the drama unfolding. Even ice cream and burger vans turned up to serve them. It was like a carnival with human tragedy as the main attraction, very harrowing to report on. My appearance must have been confusing for viewers who had last seen me doing comedy sketches with Ken Dodd. It was an example of the versatility that was needed in the early days of ITV. That evening I was back on screen in my announcing role. Business as usual. All Sundays seemed long in those days, this one more than most.

Reporting from Stockport Air Disaster

CHAPTER 7

To Thames and Anglia

NINETEEN Sixty-Seven was the Summer of Love, of Scott Mackenzie and Haight-Ashbury, San Francisco. It was also the summer the government outlawed the pirate radio stations. To appease the millions of fans who loved them, it instructed the BBC to create a pop music station, Radio 1. I had high hopes that, having done so many music shows for the BBC's Light Programme, I might be involved. I didn't think the BBC would sign up lots of the pirates. They were illegal, weren't they? How naive of me. How disappointed I was not to be in the line-up for the picture on the steps of All Souls Church next to Broadcasting House. I had been given the task of hosting the last week of *Housewives' Choice*, a show that had run on the Light Programme since 1946.

I virtually buried the Light Programme since on the final day, September 29, I also hosted *Music Through Midnight*. I felt like an undertaker. While the cool DJs of the day were pumping out the chart hits on Radio 1, I was offered *The Golden Sounds of Frank Chacksfield* on Radio 2. Frank was a nice bloke, and his music very melodic, but I was reading out requests for octogenarians and I wasn't yet thirty.

To make up for the disappointment of not being on the Radio 1 team, there were weekly trips to Tyne-Tees for the quiz series *The Bright Sparks* and a pilot for

Anglia TV for a show called *Try for Ten*. *Try for Ten* was devised by Roy Ward Dickson, a prolific quiz show creator. As with many successful quizzes, the format was fairly simple, and involved the host giving contestants statements that were either true or false. Ten correct answers would win them the modest jackpot; three wrong in a row and they were eliminated.

The pilot was well received and we began recording a 26-week series in October 1967. Anglia TV was an ambitious company and was attempting to extend its area from just the heartlands, Norfolk and Suffolk, south to Essex, west to Bedfordshire and north as far as Yorkshire and Humberside. The shows were done weekly as Outside Broadcasts with me as the host, a guest star and a hostess. It was on *Try for Ten* that I worked for the first time with my broadcasting hero Pete Murray, one of our star guests. The original hostess was the daughter of the chef at Anglia Television. She was a pretty girl but not too good at the repartee. After 13 weeks she was replaced by a professional hostess, Carol Dilworth from *The Golden Shot*. After working with Bob Monkhouse, Carol was brilliant at the comedy stuff but spent most of the rehearsals talking about her 'tremelo', who turned out to be Len Chip Hawkes. Not long afterwards they married, and Carol is now the mother of 'The One And Only' Chesney Hawkes.

There was a second series of *Doddy's Music Box* in 1968, leading to more appearances with the Squire of Knotty Ash and some on my own, in particular opening new branches of Tesco around the country. I had also made my first appearance at a disco, or discotheques as they were called then: the Pink Parrot in Liverpool.

There would probably have been a third series with Doddy had there not been a shake-up of the ITV companies later that year. ABC was due to move out of the North and Midlands and merge with Rediffusion to form Thames TV, the weekday contractor in London. It was an uncertain time for everyone, but as the year progressed it appeared that ABC would be the dominant partner and that their announcers – Philip Elsmore, Sheila Kennedy and I – would be offered the same jobs in London. This meant my Sheila uprooting from her home city and the proximity of her family and moving with the children and me to the London area.

On my working trips to the South I started looking for a suitable house. I began in Wimbledon, which I knew from my time there with my father and Delia. It was ridiculously expensive so I kept driving down the A3 until I took a left-hand turning and found a leafy village called Oxshott. There I discovered a lovely detached house on a private estate that seemed ideal. From our modest bungalow in Marple we would add an extra storey and a big back garden for the children to play in, with a weeping willow and a stream running through it.

First there were goodbyes to be said. I was sad to be leaving Manchester where so much had happened, where I made my TV and radio debuts, where Jane and David were born and sad for Sheila to be saying goodbye to her family. I wrote and presented the final programme, *Goodbye From ABC*, looking back at 12 years of one of the pioneering TV stations with clips from some of the outstanding shows. It went out on Sunday 28 July 1968. The following day, removal vans took all our belongings from Marple to Oxshott and on the Tuesday, 30 July, I was on the screen on the opening night of the new Thames Television. Ironically, the studios were in Television House in Kingsway where I did my first job as a messenger boy for ATV in 1955.

The opening night of Thames was a disaster. Striking technicians pulled the plug on the *Tommy Cooper Show* and refused to transmit it. I had to say, "Ladies and gentlemen, we apologise for the loss of the advertised programme for reasons beyond our control. We will now play you some music." For an hour there was nothing but music and a caption on the screen. What a calamitous start to the much-heralded new TV station. Before long, the strike spread to the rest of the ITV network. Instead of local programming, there was one national network manned by executives and featuring a chosen team of announcers operating from studios in Foley Street. I was one of the team along with a pal of mine, John Duncanson. He handed over to me one evening, "And now over to, if not a better man, certainly an older one – David Hamilton."

"The boys are having fun," said one of the execs. They were having fun, too, being back among the action.

Despite this inauspicious start, Thames went on to become a highly successful company, producing top light entertainment shows, top drama and excellent

Ringmaster in ITV's Christmas Circus

documentary series like *The World At War*, narrated by Sir Laurence Olivier.

From the start it was clear they were going to use me more than ABC had. I hosted Thames' first outside broadcast, *Fashion From Woburn*, then *The Magic Circle Show*. To make up for losing out on *World of Sport*, they gave me *Easter Holiday Sport* and *Whit Monday Sport* to host in 1969. Later, I would be the ringmaster in the Christmas and Easter circuses, the host of beauty contests like *Miss TV Times* and for two years the compere of the TV Times Gala Awards, then the biggest awards show on ITV. All this was in the future.

In 1970, Thames moved out of Kingsway to brand new studios in Euston Road. The big light entertainment shows continued to be produced at the former ABC studios in Teddington with their wonderful riverside setting.

Luckily, Sheila loved her new home and we found good local schools for Jane and David. Anglia Television were planning a second 26-week series of *Try for Ten* and the producer, Peter Joy, came to see me at our new home. "Carol Dilworth isn't available this time," he told me. "But we've got a new hostess for you. She's got long red hair and a great sense of humour. You'll love her." We'll see about that, I thought. Whenever anybody tells me I'm going to love someone, I'm always suspicious. It sounds too good to be true.

I met Roz Early on the platform at Liverpool Street station on the way to our first show at Long Melford near Bury St Edmunds. She was sitting on her case, waiting for me, wearing what she later told me was her sister's fur coat. As she stood up and walked towards me, I would swear I fell in love. She was absolutely brilliant on the show. After that, I picked her up every Thursday from her parents' home in Streatham and drove her to the venue. I couldn't wait for Thursdays to come round. I loved doing the shows, but most of all I couldn't wait to see her. As two people working on a show we couldn't have got on better. Sometimes in our business people are thrown together who don't really like each other. We were the opposite of that – result, a very happy show.

Anglia were a great company to work for and it was fun discovering new towns around the area. After the show we would have dinner with the crew and, unless it was a really long journey, we'd drive back, singing songs to keep awake. I'd drop her in Streatham and arrive home in the small hours of the morning. On the last night of the series we got up to dance and I said, "It'll be strange not seeing you next week." She agreed. I asked if I should pick her up as usual. "That would be nice," she said. So I carried on collecting her on Thursdays and, with no shows to do, the inevitable happened. We became lovers.

I don't feel good writing this. In fact, it seems pretty shabby: having a wife who had uprooted home with two young children and me conducting an affair with another woman. I couldn't help myself. I was helplessly in love with Roz. It was as though I had met the perfect person for me.

Carl Gresham, the agent, was still getting me lots of appearances in the North of England. Roz nicknamed him 'Mr Cash-Register Eyes' and noticed that whenever

Roz and I on Try For Ten

anyone mentioned money his eyes lit up, he rubbed his hands with glee and went red in the face. While I was in Manchester getting a new suit from Abe Sacks, the tailor, Abe suggested I join him in the ranks of racehorse owners. A visit was arranged to Percy Allden's stables in Newmarket where I was introduced to a two-year-old filly. To my untrained eye, she was a good-looking horse. Taken in by a pretty face again. The suggestion was made that I should have a half-ownership with Percy but she could run in my colours and my name and I could choose her name. The colours I chose were green with pink cross belts. As Newmarket was in the Anglia TV region, I suggested we call her 'Try for Ten' after the TV show. When Roz and I were next in the area we dropped into the stables and posed for pictures for *TV Times* and the *Daily Mirror*. The horse loved polo mints and every time she was given one, she displayed a fine set of teeth. Very photogenic.

When it came to running she wasn't quite so good. Unplaced in her first race at Leicester, the jockey, Frankie Durr, said she dwelt at the gate. She had a habit of doing that. I couldn't get to all her meetings but reports from Percy told me that while the others were haring off at the start she was day-dreaming. When she got going she was a fast runner, but over short distances there was too much ground to make up. One meeting I did get to was at the old track at Alexandra Park. At Ally Pally she flew off at the start but there was a dip in the track where you couldn't see the horses from the grandstand. As they were going into the first bend she was doing quite well. The horses disappeared into the dip and came out in a completely different order. Very perplexing. Maybe 'Try for Ten' wasn't trying.

The horse had run unplaced nine times so when she

ran at her home track, Newmarket, on the last day of the season, Roz and I went along with low expectations and certainly weren't having a bet on her. We were watching the race in the bar when suddenly we heard the commentator say the magic words, "And in the lead it's 'Try for Ten'." We raced down to the rails to get a closer view. Heading towards us I could see the green and pink cross belts worn by the jockey, Stan Smith, but the horse appeared to be looking round, waiting for her friends to pass her. She just wasn't used to being in front, but more familiar with looking at other horses' backsides. In the end, 'Try for Ten' on her tenth run came in third at 33-1. Never was a third place so celebrated. That night we took Percy and his wife Edna out for a slap-up dinner in Cambridge.

No wonder they call horse racing the Sport of Kings. As I discovered that summer, it's an expensive business. As for my half-share in the horse, I must have had the front half that did all the eating. After the meeting at Newmarket, Percy Allden retired. 'Try for Ten', apparently, was

Roz and I with Try For Ten, the racehorse

sold to America. Stan Smith, the jockey, retired after a career riding much better horses than mine, and I most certainly retired as an owner. It must be the only race in history after which owner, trainer, jockey and horse all retired.

CHAPTER 8

Have-a-Go Hamilton

INEVITABLY, Sheila found out about Roz. She'd suspected something for a long time because she said I seemed to be so happy. I moved out of the house and rented a flat in Gloucester Road for what I said would be a trial separation. Early in 1970 my mother was taken ill. As with my father, the diagnosis was lung cancer. Once again, the doctor advised me not to tell her, but armed with the experience of what had happened to my father, I'm sure she knew. Back then, there seemed to be no treatment that would make patients better or at least prolong their lives. I was told she had six months and that turned out to be the case, and she spent much of her remaining time in Guy's Hospital. She died at the age of 58. It was a short life but for much of the time a happy one. She loved her visits to the countryside and the farm where she grew up. She loved and was loved by two men, my father and Jack, who I suspect was the love of her life. I admired the way she survived the loss of Jack by carving out a career in her forties. When she died she left me £5000 in her will, the only money I've ever been given in my life. It was hard-earned money and I vowed to her I wouldn't waste it. No more racehorses.

She was a sitting tenant at the flat in Fulham and after she died I inherited the tenancy and Roz and I moved in. This time we moved into the main bedroom which wasn't as damp as my pokey bedroom, but the flat was still pretty basic, with the bath still in the kitchen and with the hot and cold running mice coming in from the Thames nearby. We sunbathed by the river in Bishops Park, watching the boats go by and walked through the park to watch Fulham playing at Craven Cottage on Saturday afternoons. One day I spotted who I thought was Marc Bolan driving his Rolls Royce up Fulham Road and said to myself, "That's a star's car and that's what I'm going to buy." So I did. There we were living in a pokey little flat with a Rolls Royce parked around the corner. Fur coat and no knickers.

In the space of three years, my marriage had broken up and I'd lost both my parents, each of them in their 50s. Once again, the only way to numb the pain was to throw myself into work. The next stop on my tour of the regional TV stations was Plymouth. Westward TV offered me a quiz show series called *Dig and Run* and then a beauty contest series, *Miss Westward*. I did a few *Radio 1 Clubs* from the BBC's Paris Theatre in Lower Regent Street, an intimate venue where I interviewed lots of pop stars, supporting the main DJ. Radio was

In a BBC studio in the early 1970s

my first love but my radio career seemed to be going nowhere very much, when out of the blue came a call from a Radio 2 producer, Tony Luke, asking if I would do a demo for a show called *Late Night Extra*. *LNE* had a different host every night, Monday to Friday, and Tony Luke had earlier discovered a young Irish broadcaster and gave a broadcasting debut to one Terry Wogan. By 1970, Wogan had moved on to a daily show and the *LNE* line up was: Bob Holness on Monday nights, Brian Matthew on Tuesday, my old pal John Benson on Wednesday, Peter Latham on Thursday and now I was to become the Friday night host of the show that was heard on Radio 1 and Radio 2. Friday suited me well. It had a good feel about it. As they used to say on *Ready Steady Go*, the weekend starts here. *LNE* was more than just a music show as it included guests, often actors who would drop in after the curtain came down on their shows in London. Peter Sellers, who I had been warned could be difficult, was an absolute joy, setting the scene for our interview: "Here I am within the portals of the BBC with my colleague Hugh Jampton," a cunning piece of rhyming slang.

When producer Ian Fenner and I were despatched to the Dorchester Hotel to interview the film star Charlton Heston, we were escorted to his suite on the top floor. Greeting us was a man mountain, 6ft 3 and built like a brick outhouse. "Would you care for a drink?" he asked. I declined, remembering my golden rule of never drinking before working. Ian Fenner accepted and Charlton Heston poured him a huge tumbler of whisky. The great man turned out to be a brilliant interviewee: witty, articulate and a great teller of stories about his movie adventures. We got 30 minutes of terrific material in the can. Interview over, he asked if we would like another drink. Fenner said "Yes," and Heston poured another full tumbler... As we chatted away, he said to Ian, "As a matter of interest, does the BBC pay for this kind of thing?" Fenner coughed into his whisky and said, "There will be a nominal fee."

"Howd'ya mean, nominal?" said Heston.

Fenner coughed nervously again and said to the star of so many biblical epics, "Ten guineas."

"Couldn't you just give me a tie?" said the big man. More nervous coughs from the producer while explaining that unfortunately the BBC couldn't pay in ties. How careful the Beeb was with its money in those days. Terry Wogan's first fee for hosting *Late Night Extra* was £33. How things change.

Tony Luke came up with the idea that I should do a feature for *LNE* called 'Have-a-Go Hamilton' where, armed with a portable tape recorder, I should learn to do dangerous things. Were they trying to kill me off?, I wondered. First, I flew a Tiger Moth. Well, the pilot flew it, sitting behind me in the open cockpit with me taking the controls for a while. Then it was a glider – more frightening this time with no engine, gliding across the M40 into Booker aerodrome near Marlow. The next outing was in a hot air balloon from Dunstable Flying Club, a joint effort with the 'Action Girl' from the *Sun* newspaper. It was like no other kind of flying, suspended in the air with no noise apart from the sound of dogs barking up at us as we cruised over the town of Leighton Buzzard. A bumpy landing, though, as the basket hit the ground, all described later on *Late Night Extra*.

In 1970, when speedway racing returned to Wembley Stadium, Ed Stewart and I were invited to do the MC-ing: shades of my boyhood days with Auntie Gertie. Though crowds were not as big in the '70s, it was still great to see the sport back at the Twin Towers. Throughout the season the promoters joked that on the final night there should be a challenge race between Ed and me. "We'll do it on pushbikes," I said. "Let's have a donkey race," said Ed. But they insisted we did it on proper speedway bikes and, as the last night drew nearer, they suggested we bring a couple of pals to make up the usual number of four riders. We came up with a couple of guys we played football with – Leapy Lee, who'd just had a chart hit with 'Little Arrows', and Troy Dante, whose main claim to fame was that he was living with Diana Dors.

The last meeting of the season was Great Britain versus the Rest of the World, and a good crowd turned out to see some of the world's finest riders. We were told to be there for practice at 6 o'clock ahead of the meeting start at 7.30. Incredibly, some of the riders lent us their bikes and leathers. What were they thinking of? We could have wrecked their valuable equipment. Troy Dante claimed to have ridden a speedway bike at Wimbledon, but I had never ridden a motorbike before and had no idea of how to make it go. It was explained to me that the throttle was on the right handlebar and the clutch on the left. Let the clutch out slowly, they said, and tickle the throttle. Don't do it too sharply or the bike will lift up and throw you off. We were told the start was the most dangerous part, so rather than lining up at the tapes we would have a rolling start where we'd be pushed off and go from there. I would have a tape recorder strapped to my chest and commentate on the race to listeners of *Late Night Extra* as we did four laps of the circuit.

At the end of the night, after the big meeting was over, we donned our leathers, steel boots and crash helmets, mounted our borrowed bikes and prepared to race. My plan was to stay at the back, try to keep up with the others and describe the race from there. I had no intention to be a hero, merely to stay alive, a rank amateur in one of the world's most dangerous sports. If I stayed at the back, nobody would knock me off or run me over. As I was pushed out of the pits, I noticed the others were lined up at the tapes. There must have been a change of plan and nobody had told me. Perhaps they said they were confident to start in the normal way. There was I heading towards the tapes which were down and with no brakes I had no idea how to stop. Seeing me coming, the referee raised the tapes at the last minute and, worst possible scenario, I headed into the first bend in the lead. One by one they passed me. Troy Dante, really turning the throttle on, crashed into the safety fence. I think the others came to grief as well. As I finished the race,

At Wimbledon speedway, 1970s

someone handed me an onion as a prize. When I asked what the race time was, I was told just over 60 seconds which sounded pretty good until I was told, "That was for one lap." The slowest speedway race ever. At the end of it my arms were aching and I had more admiration than ever for the guys who do it for a living.

My next dangerous assignment was to wrestle with Jackie Pallo, one of the bad guys of the grunt and groan business. On the way to the gym in South London, Chris Serle, the producer, said, "Tell him it's all a sham. No one actually gets hurt." Like a mug I took his advice. Pallo threw me round the ring: with the odd cross buttock and forearm smash, I thought he was going to break every bone in my body. "You think it's a sham, do you?" he asked as we climbed out of the ring. I was too breathless to answer. No wonder Mick McManus didn't like him very much. Thanks a bunch, Chris.

Chris Serle later became a TV star and did a series called *In at the Deep End* where he learned to do dangerous things. A sort of 'Have-a-Go Hamilton' on television. Fancy that.

While I was doing *Late Night Extra*, Sheila took the kids on holiday to Malta and liked it so much she decided to stay there. I flew out to visit them for a few days and noticed that Jane and David were speaking with a broken English accent, like the local kids. It upset me a lot that my kids were so far away. In the flight on the way back I had to lock myself in the lavatory for a few minutes to let the tears flow. The next day I was back on stage at the *Radio 1 Club*. The show goes on.

When I moved South, the invitation had come to join the Top Ten XI football team. Back in the '60s there were no professional matches on Sundays, but showbiz matches were allowed because they were organised for charity. Sunday was a dead day; nothing happened. The idea was that we would all go to church and then enjoy a day of rest. Because it was such a dead day, big crowds turned up to watch a bunch of showbusiness people kicking a ball around. Ed Stewart was the goalkeeper and captain of the Top Ten XI and regular players included Dave Dee, Junior Campbell from the band Marmalade and the songwriter Barry Mason. The best-known team was the Showbiz XI and after a while I joined them, along with the likes of Tommy Steele, Ray and Dave Davies from The Kinks, and later even Rod Stewart.

On the ball with the Showbiz XI

Travelling to the matches was always fun with the anticipation of the game ahead, and there was lots of horseplay. Often we travelled by coach. There were boxes of wine which we called leaking handbags and which were devoured on the way back home. Roz and I stuck mostly to tea. Occasionally we did the trips by train. On one trip from Paddington to Exeter Ray Davies and Larry Taylor, who did the stunts for James Bond in the movies, acted out a little scenario to the amusement of the other chaps sitting at tables nearby. Seated opposite a couple of ladies of a certain age, they put their hands on the table to reveal they were handcuffed to each other. As their conversation progressed, it turned out that Ray was a convict returning to Exeter gaol and that Larry was the warder charged with getting him there.

"If you spring me, there could be a lot of money in it for you," suggested Ray. The ladies were agog.

"More than my job's worth," said Larry.

"I'm talking serious money here."

"How could it be done?"

"We have a scuffle on the train. I get the key out of your pocket and I do a runner."

Negotiations continued through the journey. The old ladies sat there in silence while the rest of the team

Rod Stewart, on the extreme right. stretches a leg with the Showbiz XI, including Tommy Steele and Bill Oddie

were struggling to supress our mirth. When we got off the train at Exeter, with Ray and Larry still handcuffed to each other, we looked back and the old ladies were chattering away furiously. They had plenty to talk about for the rest of their journey. More laughs would follow with the Showbiz XI, more matches with big crowds on league grounds, many with or against some of Britain's finest footballers.

CHAPTER 9

Smile (Though Your Heart Is Aching)

MIKE Yarwood was a brilliant impressionist, his party piece being his take on Harold Wilson, but his best impression – reserved for his friends in the business – was of his agent Dave Forrester in a telephone call trying to sell Ken Dodd and the Diddy Men – to producers in America. "No, they're not fucking midgets."

Dave Forrester was the archetypal North Country show business agent. His number 1 client was Ken Dodd and after the first series of *Doddy's Music Box*, Ken suggested he should represent me as well. One of the first pieces of advice Dave Forrester gave me was, "Take everything that's going, even if it's only a number 8 bus." It was advice I never forgot. In 1971 Dave came up with my first pantomime appearance in *Cinderella* in Bradford. The role of Buttons, the page boy, was quite a challenging one and I explained to Dave Forrester my reservations. "I can't sing or dance and I'm not an actor."

"Minor details," said the veteran agent. Off I went on what would be a long run, opening on Christmas Eve and with extensions running for nine weeks after that. It meant giving up *Late Night Extra* and Thames for over two months, but both said they would have me back immediately the run was over.

People said I would hate Bradford but the opposite

was true. Roz auditioned for a role in the chorus, which she got, and we rented a house in Tong, not far from the town centre but with horses grazing in a neighbouring field. We both fell in love with the Bradford Alhambra, a beautiful old theatre with its terracotta turrets. I was second on the bill to John Hanson who played the Prince, fresh from his success in *The Desert Song*. (Hence all the jokes about the sand in his dressing room.) John had a tremendous following and coachloads of his fans descended on the Alhambra from all over the North of England.

When rehearsals began, it became clear it was going to be a heavy workload: two shows most days and only Sundays off. At the same time I was presenting a children's series for Yorkshire TV called *Just Look*, so once a week I drove to Leeds to record the show. Luckily, I was working with a very friendly cast, all seasoned professionals, aware that it was my first panto and willing to give me any advice they could. I became particularly friendly with the Broker's Men, Wally Lester and Keith Smart – just as well, as they joined me in an acrobatic sketch where I hung upside down on black wires in front of a black curtain while they appeared to throw

Buttons with Ken Dodd

me around and catch me. The wires were attached to a very uncomfortable harness which the camp wardrobe man seemed to take rather too much pleasure in fitting every day. My up and down movements were controlled by one of the stage hands pulling on a rope from the wings. Too violent a jerk could have a nasty effect on the orchestra stalls, if you get my meaning. It was a very dangerous act. If the rope had slipped through his hands, I could have plummeted head first onto the stage. He wore a thick pair of gloves, and I bought him a drink every night – after the show.

As Bradford was Carl Gresham's home town, we saw quite a bit of 'Mr Cash-Register Eyes'. For my song sheet spot where I got the kids up on stage, he suggested I do the song 'Travel Inter City like the Boys Do'. He said everybody knew the words of it from the TV commercial. Looking back now, I wonder what on earth I was doing getting them to sing a TV commercial rather than a classic like 'There's a Worm at the Bottom of the Garden and His Name Is Wiggly Woo'. Did people think I was getting free rail tickets? I wasn't. Or was Carl? The rascal. I never found out.

One afternoon I had an unexpected visitor. There was a knock on my dressing room door and standing there was Ken Dodd. I didn't know he'd been in the audience for the matinee. "Come on, I'll take you out for dinner," he said, a nice surprise as Ken was known as being a bit careful. We went across the road to Goldsack's fish and chip shop. It was unlicensed but Ken walked into the back parlour, took two bottles of lager out of his overcoat pockets and said to the woman behind the counter, "Cod and chips twice, love." As we ate the cod and chips, he gave me some advice on how to play Buttons (and he'd been a brilliant Buttons). "You've got the bubbly bit, but you've got to work on the pathos," he said. "You've got to remember Cinderella is basically a cow. She's interested in the Prince because he's got lots of money but she really loves you, the little page boy." He then suggested ways in which I could add to the pathos. He also recommended I buy a radio mic that I could fit into my costume. "You're on a long run in the winter and could easily lose your voice. To save you having to get on to the front riser all the time, get your own microphone." I took his advice.

Where the pathos was concerned a couple of nights later I rang Ken to say that after the kitchen scene where I sang 'Smile', the old Charlie Chaplin song, to Cinderella, a little boy in the front row called out, "Cinders, marry Buttons."

"Well done, son," said Ken. "You're on your way."

As for the microphone, it made a big difference, but one night it did catch me out. The battery part had an On-Off switch and fitted into a pocket at the back of my trousers. As I came off stage for a costume change, I switched it to what I thought was Off but, in fact, was On. John Hanson, as the Prince, was making his entrance on stage to be greeted by his subjects. "Hark, I hear voices from the forest," he said. At which point the camp wardrobe man's voice bellowed out to the audience, "No wonder Cinderella runs off with the Prince. For God's sake, be butch." "Fuck off," said Buttons, the children's new favourite.

That apart, Ken's advice was invaluable. I thought about it afterwards and considered would I have rather gone to the best restaurant in town and talked about holidays and football or had fish and chips and priceless advice from the master? As people say today, a no-brainer.

After the last show on the last night, Roz and I sat in the stalls, soaking up the atmosphere of the marvellous Bradford Alhambra. It was as though we knew we would never be back there again, which turned out to be right.

The following year, 1972, the old flesh peddler Dave Forrester booked me into another pantomime – this time a touring one with a shorter run. Little and Large were my co-stars in *Red Riding Hood*, and the itinerary was two weeks in Doncaster, followed by a week in Hanley and a week in Gloucester. Roz auditioned for and got the part of Fairy Kindheart. As we were touring, I decided to hire a Dormobile. We drove up to Doncaster in a pea-souper fog. I had arranged to park at Doncaster Airport and found what appeared to be the car park. Early in the morning we were woken by someone furiously banging on the door and telling us to move right away as we were on the runway and a plane was attempting to land.

Once again, the panto meant a break from Thames TV and *Late Night Extra*, although I did do an *LNE* show from the dressing room after the opening night's show. A few weeks before *Red Riding Hood* opened, the BBC came up with an offer I couldn't refuse. Radio 2 asked me to stand in for Terry Wogan on the breakfast show on the first week of 1973. For a week this was my blistering schedule: Matinee and evening show at Doncaster; quick change and then taxi to Leeds station; sleeper to London; taxi to Broadcasting House; breakfast show at Radio 2; taxi to King's Cross; train to Doncaster; repeat for four more days. 'Sleeper' turned out to be a misnomer. By the end of the week I was like a zombie. Although I was topping the bill, the panto wasn't as good as the one at Bradford. Instead of the wonderful role of Buttons, I was playing Red Riding Hood's brother, a nothing part. I did have one good scene in the second half where I read

Ye Olde News At Ten which I had written on a piece of parchment.

"A man was knocked over in Doncaster city centre today by a steamroller. He's now in wards 8, 9 and 10 of the Doncaster Royal Infirmary."

"A gang of thieves broke into Doncaster police station and stole the lavatory seats. A police spokesman said we have nothing to go on."

"George Best has just announced his retirement from active football. He'll never play active football again. He's just signed on for Doncaster Rovers."

It went well for a few nights until suddenly the George Best joke seemed to be dying.

One evening I came down early to watch some of Syd and Eddie's act from the wings. "Have you heard about George Best?" said Eddie. "Just announced his retirement from active football. Just signed on for Doncaster Rovers." Never trust a comic.

Soon after I got back to London, Douglas Muggeridge, the Controller of Radio 1 and 2, asked to see me.

This sounds promising, I thought. I'd been standing in for the likes of Terry Wogan, Pete Murray and Jimmy Young. Now it looked as though I might be getting my own daily show, something I'd hoped for since Radios 1 and 2 launched six years before. When we met, Douglas felt I might be more suited to Radio 2 but Radio 1 was the more exciting station, the one that played the pop music of the day and that was where I wanted to be. I didn't have to wait long. In the early Spring Derek Chinnery, the boss of Radio 1, called me to his office and told me that in a big shake up Jimmy Young was moving to Radio 2 and that Tony Blackburn and I would be the first people to have three-hour daily shows, Monday to Friday. Mine would be in the afternoon between 2 and

5 pm, following Johnnie Walker. It seemed too good to be true, and at our next meeting I realised it was. A third of my show would be non-needle time – in other words, tapes recorded at BBC studios rather than records which were what everyone wanted to hear. I'd worry about the specifics later, I thought. For now let's grab the opportunity.

Looking back now, those five years between 1968 and 1973 when I returned to London were a magical time for me with that feeling of bubbling under, travelling the country, getting known, waiting for the big chance to come along. I had certainly not been an overnight success but someone beavering away, learning his trade and hoping the right chance would happen. When it did I appreciated it even more and was determined to make the most of it.

Doing a daily show on Radio 1 meant giving up *Late Night Extra*. Tony Luke put together a 'Goodbye' show for me with a live audience at the BBC's Playhouse Theatre near the embankment in Charing Cross, with guest stars including Sacha Distel and Roy Hudd. For once I was overwhelmed and quite nervous despite the fact there was a lovely, warm audience. Roy Hudd broke the ice when he came on stage and dropped his trousers. It got such a laugh that everything went fine after that. I was a great fan of Roy and his wonderful radio show *The News Huddlines*. The real pros know the right thing to do at the right time. I was sad to be leaving LNE and grateful to Tony Luke who took me on when I was out of fashion at BBC radio, but I knew Radio 1 was the place to be. Roz was there at the show, of course, and looked after guests in the green room, including Delia, who had come along to see the boy who terrorised her life now enjoying a moment of glory she could never have expected.

Meanwhile, Roz had been offered a summer season show with Larry Grayson in Margate, a long-running show that would take up the whole of the summer. I didn't want her to go, it would be the first time we'd been apart in four years.

"I won't go if you'll marry me," she said. Marriage had been her topic of conversation for a long time. Why couldn't I make a decision? Was somewhere in the back of my mind the thought that I didn't want any more children? From the moment she left I missed her.

The David Hamilton Show launched on Radio 1 on 4 June 1973. The first record I played was Can The Can by Suzi Quatro. It was great to be 'self-opping' – playing all the records and jingles myself – but in the early days I did make a few mistakes, once playing two records at the same time, resulting in a dreadful cacophony and once playing a Rolling Stones track that included the F-word. The technical operator, who was on the other side of the glass keeping an eye of levels, came through on the talk back saying, "Have you heard this?" I hadn't because I was too busy setting up a record on the other turntable. When I switched across I could hear Mick Jagger singing, "You're a starfucker, starfucker, star..." I hastily faded it out and went to the other disc. When I took the offending LP off the turntable, I noticed a sticker on the label saying On no account must track 4 be played. I was supposed to be playing track 3. A mistake easily made, but one not to be repeated.

I'd only been doing the show a couple of weeks when I got a dreadful toothache. A trip to the dentist revealed I had an impacted wisdom tooth, which resulted in a very painful operation to remove it. For a few days afterwards my mouth was very sore and I had difficulty speaking, hardly ideal for the new host of a daily national radio show. That, combined with missing Roz, made me very under the weather.

I became good friends with Peter Walker, the film producer, after he invited me to appear in his film, *Tiffany Jones*, that starred the beautiful Anoushka Hempel. In the film I played myself (not difficult) as a news presenter interviewing the actor Eric Pohlmann. It was Peter who suggested we go to see Roz in her show at Margate. She looked great on stage and that night when we stayed at a hotel in Broadstairs I told her how much I missed her and that I would ask Sheila for a divorce so that we could get married. She said, "I'll be counting the days until the end of the season." She came home for a Sunday a couple of weeks later and when I again broached the subject, she said, "I don't want to talk about it any more."

"But for four years you've talked about it regularly," I said, to which she replied that she wasn't sure anymore. "When will you be sure?" I asked.

"I'll tell you at the end of the summer season."

I decided to leave her alone, not pester her, give her time to think. I had plenty to keep me busy.

Before I signed up to do the radio show, speedway racing had come into my life again. Reg Fearman, the ex-speedway rider turned promoter, had asked me to be the MC for his track at Reading. On Monday afternoons, after my radio show finished at five, I drove through the rush hour from London to the stadium in Tilehurst in time for the meeting build-up at 7. Reg was a canny businessman, had built a strong team and the stadium was packed to the rafters every Monday night. Part of the deal was that I would take a celebrity guest with me every week. Often they were glamorous young actresses.

Anders Michanek, the Reading Racers' Swedish ace, would take them for a lap of the track on his bike at the end of the meeting. The girls loved it because Anders was very handsome, Anders loved it because the girls were pretty and Reg Fearman loved it because it always made a nice photo spread in *Speedway Star* magazine and in the *Reading Evening Post*. Pop stars like Peter Skellern and Lyn Paul, from the New Seekers, came along. We even had an appearance from one of the biggest stars of the time, Gary Glitter, who was number 1 in the charts with 'I'm the Leader of the Gang', very appropriately a motorbikers' song. Glitter was charging thousands of pounds for appearances in the '70s, but his record company, Bell Records, persuaded him to do it for nothing as a goodwill gesture to a Radio 1 DJ who would be playing his records. After a big introduction from me, he drove round the track in his Rolls Royce. The reception he got wasn't at all what he expected and the crowd booed him loudly. I was told later that it was because for the only time that season Reading lost at Tilehurst and the crowd thought he was an unlucky omen. Years later, I reflected that perhaps they knew something I didn't.

Glitter was the one hitch of the season. Reading won the British League and my reward on the last night was to have the riders throw bags of flour over me, a final night custom for a championship winning team, I was assured. Reg Fearman, standing nearby, escaped without a fleck on his suit. He was even smarter than I'd thought.

CHAPTER 10

To Radio 1

THE Radio 1 team of 1973 was the last line-up before the launch of legalised commercial radio in the UK.

The original team from 1967 had enjoyed the glory days when, apart from Radio Luxembourg with its dodgy signal in the evening, there was no other pop music station. Now, with commercial radio on the horizon, the class of '73 was charged with hanging on to its huge audience. The line-up was Noel Edmonds on breakfast, followed by Tony Blackburn, who had moved reluctantly to 9am – Noon, Johnnie Walker at lunchtime, with me from 2–5pm. The first commercial stations, Capital (music) and LBC (talk), launched in October 1973, followed gradually by stations in every town and city in the country. Unlike the BBC, the commercial stations were run by businessmen and would have to be successful or they would go out of business and, unlike Radio 1, they could concentrate on their own patch with local travel and weather. All of them could pitch their programmes directly against the Radio 1 schedules and they didn't have the same needle time problems. Inevitably, they would chip away at Radio 1's audience and the only way 1's listening figures could go was down. Although name DJs like Kenny Everett and Dave Cash would defect to Capital where they had more freedom, for most aspiring DJs Radio 1 was still the place to be.

Hardly was the ink dry on the Radio 1 contract than Thames offered me the role of co-hosting with Judith Chalmers a new holiday travel series called *Wish You Were Here*. I had to turn it down because I was needed in the radio studio five days a week. As it turned out, *Wish You Were Here* ran for nearly 30 years, during which Judith got to see the loveliest parts of the world and had the best suntan in the business. So much in our profession is to do with luck, timing and being in the right place at the right time. This was a case of really bad timing but, though I missed out on a long running TV series, I knew that radio was my first love.

As the daily show got under way, lots of other doors opened. There was a daily breakfast show on the BBC World Service and inflight recordings for British Airways, Monarch and other airlines. For some time I'd been recording promotional tapes – often for record companies but for other organisations, too – for former record producer Chris Parmenter at his home studio in Battersea. Roz and I became friendly with Chris and his wife, singer and actress Tracy Rogers, and often after recordings the four of us would go round to the local pub. Now I had a Radio 1 show the number of recordings increased. Then there were the discos. Radio 1 DJs were doing them all over Britain, some with special lighting and dancers. Unlike today, when DJs are paid a fortune to mix records without speaking, we were expected to put together some kind of act. The offers came flooding in. One night I'd be in Plymouth, the next Aberdeen. Unless it was a weekend, I was always back in London for the radio show the next day.

To welcome Roz back from her long summer season, I had organised on a Sunday in September two tickets to see Johnny Mathis at the London Palladium, but first there was the business of her long-awaited decision.

"I'm moving back to my mother's," she told me. When I asked her if she still wanted to go to the Palladium, she said "Yes." So we sat in the stalls holding hands while Mathis sang his romantic songs. Everything seemed the same to me. It took her a week to move out. Friends rang and she told them she still loved me, but not in the way I wanted her to. What the hell did that mean?

From the moment she left, my world fell apart. Several times I reached for the phone to call her at her mother's flat. Every time, at the last moment I resisted. I just knew it wasn't the right thing to do. For a very long time I hoped she might come back. I remembered that when Ken Dodd told me about working on the pathos in *Cinderella*, I said to Roz, "I've never been in love with someone who didn't love me." Well, I was now and the thought struck me that I'd make a much better Buttons next time.

In March 1974, ATV were bringing back *Sunday Night at the London Palladium* for a seven-week run and invited me to do the voice-over at the start – "Tonight from the London Palladium..." – and also to warm up the audience before the show. Word reached me that Roz would be on the show as one of the Second Generation dancers. I couldn't just bump into her in the wings. It would be too painful, so I finally picked up the phone and spoke to her for the first time in six months. She agreed it would be weird to meet again like that and said she would have lunch with me.

We met at the restaurant in Syon Park where plumed birds walked among the tables, a park we'd discovered on a memorable boat trip a couple of years before. After a long lunch, we drove to Battersea to see our friends

Chris and Tracy Parmenter. When Roz went to the loo, Tracy said to me, "Everything seems the same." I showed Roz a flat I was buying in Hallam Street, a short walk from the BBC. She made some suggestions about things I might do with it. I hoped that the thought of getting away from that dreadful dark and damp flat in Fulham might tempt her to come back.

What a pleasure it was to tread the boards for the first time at the London Palladium, even if it was only as the show's warm-up man. It is a very special theatre: a good size, yet intimate. During the afternoon I would sit in the stalls watching rehearsals. One day, Clodagh Rodgers was due to appear but taken ill and at the last minute a replacement act was found. Three girls from America bounded on stage and sang a song called 'Year of Decision'. It was around the time Diana Ross was leaving The Supremes, and I thought to myself that these could be the new Supremes, though they were not from Detroit but Philadelphia. The following morning, I spoke to my Radio 1 producer and asked if he had seen *Sunday Night at the London Palladium*. When he said No, I said,

With The Three Degrees

"Well, millions of people did and will have heard this song." I asked him to change my Record of the Week – the 'Hamilton Hotshot', as I called it – to 'Year of Decision'. He listened to the record and agreed with me that it was a winner. Thus was born the first chart hit for The Three Degrees.

When we found new artists we tended to stick with them, following their story as it were. The Three Degrees' follow-up, and their next 'Hamilton Hotshot', was 'When Will I See You Again?'. This one went global, was number 1 in 25 different countries and became a multi-million seller. When it sold the magic million, the record company, Philadelphia Records, asked me to present the girls with a gold disc at their stage show at the Victoria Apollo. On cue I walked out on stage and said to the audience, "I'm here to tell you that 'When Will I See You Again?' has sold a million copies." The place erupted. I handed the gold disc to the lead singer Sheila Ferguson, the band struck up and the girls broke into the song. I watched from the wings. They never sang it better. Later Prince Charles danced with Sheila Ferguson and said, "The Three Degrees are my favourite group," so they became By Royal Appointment. But I found them first, and it all began on *Sunday Night at the London Palladium*.

When the series was over, I invited Roz out again. This time a record company had invited me to join them in a box at the Royal Albert Hall to see Andy Williams. Like Johnny Mathis before, Andy sang his romantic songs but this time there was no holding hands. Roz seemed more interested in a pal she'd seen. I felt my girl slipping away. I ran her home to her mother's place in Streatham, we had a small argument, and that was the last time I would see her. A couple of years later, I heard that she had reunited with her German lion tamer boyfriend. Before long they were married and she had moved on to her new life, living in the circus in Germany. When I spoke to her mother she said, "I can see how she fell for you. You are so like him." What? I did all that, broke up my marriage for someone who fell in love with me because I reminded her of someone else? All the hurt I must have caused Sheila I was now feeling myself. Nothing more than I deserved.

CHAPTER 11

To Hallam Street

TWO nights a week I was still doing my announcing stint at Thames. This involved quite a mad dash. Off the air at Broadcasting House at 5pm; a short drive to the flat in Hallam Street, equidistant between BH and the new Thames studios on the Euston Road; a change of clothes into suit, shirt and tie and then on to Euston for a quick visit to make up and on the air at Thames at 5.45. To be honest the announcing shifts were pretty boring, waiting around through the programmes to do 30 or 45 seconds on screen in between them, so I tried to liven up with bits of humour that occasionally got me into trouble. Talking about a *Des O'Connor Show*, I said, "On the *Des O'Connor Show* tonight there's something for everyone. For the ladies there's Des O'Connor. For the men there's Joan Collins. And for those who haven't made their minds up yet there's Lionel Blair." A couple of minutes later, the phone buzzed in the studio. On the line was Lionel.

"David, I'm very upset with you."

"Why's that, Lionel?"

"What you just said about me."

"Lionel, it's what everyone says."

"What upsets me most is I thought we were chums."

"We *are* chums," I said. "It's only your chums you can be rude about." He put down the phone, unconvinced.

Another programme that frequently cropped up on

my shift was *Crossroads*, the only soap where the sets moved more than the actors. One evening I was given the information – "Tonight an actor arrives at the Crossroads Motel." I delivered the line to camera, but out of the corner of my eye I could see I had a couple of seconds left. So the way it came out was: "Tonight an actor arrives at the Crossroads Motel – not before time." Two minutes later, the phone buzzed. At the other end was Noele Gordon, the Queen of *Crossroads*.

"I'm very upset with you, David."

"Why's that, Noele?"

"What you just said about my programme."

"But it's what everyone says."

She ended the call, once again unconvinced. She was a powerful woman with connections in high places. I didn't get told off, because *Crossroads* was an ATV production and Thames only really cared about their own shows.

One night it was I who was the butt of the humour. Linking into a film starring the actor Dana Andrews, I confused him with the actress Dana Wynter and referred to him as "the lovely Dana Andrews". Two minutes later, a call came through and on the line was an American voice.

"Mr Hamilton. My name is Al Cernik. I am a lawyer representing the actor Dana Andrews."

"Oh yes?"

"Mr Hamilton. I've just heard your broadcast and I think you have implied that my client is effeminate."

"Oh, no."

"I would go further and say that you have implied that Mr Andrews is a... homosexual."

"Oh, no," I said, spluttering by now. "What I was saying is that he is a lovely person."

"Mr Hamilton. You will be receiving a letter from me."

More grovelling from me continued, and then suddenly the voice changed to an English one. "Got you, you bugger," he said.

It was Shaw Taylor from *Police Five*, the man known as the 'Whispering Grass', who I'd been friends with since the days I wrote his scripts at ATV. Consider myself nicked! (I should have rumbled the prank, because Al Cernik was the real name of the singer Guy Mitchell.)

'Spot The Tootsie' with Bernie Winters and Henry Cooper

BBC TV were launching a new series called *Monty Python's Flying Circus* and asked if they could use me and the Thames station ident to introduce one of the shows. Thames naturally asked to be able to approve the script before releasing both. Once they gave their clearance I went to BBC Television Centre to meet John Cleese and the rest of the cast on the set of what would be a cult TV series before recording my piece, "Good evening. We've got an action-packed evening for you tonight on Thames, but right now here's a rotten old BBC programme."

Next up came another new series that would turn out to be cult viewing. I was asked to do a number of recordings as the voice on the radio in HMP Slade, the setting for *Porridge*. As I committed them to tape, it occurred to me that the inmates would probably be rude about me and turn me off. So what, I thought – it will be good exposure on a great programme.

Though the announcing job was boring, Thames started using me more in programmes. I became the regular host of beauty contests, the main one being 'Miss TV Times', ITV's big contest of the year. I was hardly the ideal host. As most of the girls were tall and wore high stilettos, I spent most of the time with their boobs at my eye level – which, come to think of it, was not such a bad thing.

With Roz gone, my private life was in a bit of a mess. I met a girl called Keira, who offered to sort out my fan mail which was piling up unanswered, not to mention bills that needed paying and cheques that needed paying into the bank. She set up an office in the flat during the day and also got me a few bookings. She was what is known these days as a friend with benefits, but neither of us wanted a complete commitment and both of us were seeing other people. At one of my appearances I bumped into a girl I had met briefly when I was with Roz and who at the time I thought was very attractive. Felicity Devonshire, the model and actress, was not unlike Roz: about the same height, though blonde. This time I took her telephone number and we started seeing each other. As she was a high-profile model and I was a high-profile

DJ, it wasn't long before the press cottoned on to us and the tabloids started splashing pictures of us together, which didn't do any harm to either of our careers.

Felicity, known to her friends as Fluff, was a high-spirited girl. She once took me for a spin on her motorbike when she hit 70 mph along Park Lane with me on the pillion hanging on for dear life. (Not to be recommended.) What we had was a fling. I was not The One for her and she was not The One for me, but it was fun at the time and probably what we both needed.

Following my work with Ken Dodd, Thames booked me for some *Benny Hill Shows*. Benny was enormously hot property at the time. He shows sold around the

ITV panto. Back row, l. to r: Hughie Green, Mike Winters, Bernard Breslaw, Bernie Winters, William G Stewart Middle row: Wendy Craig, Benny Hill, Anita Harris, Edward Woodward, Barbara Windsor, Fred Emney Front row: Ann Holloway, Sid James and DH

world, even to non-English-speaking countries. His cheeky humour translated easily into all languages. Once again I was cast as the interviewer. Benny wrote all his own scripts and often generously gave me some funny lines. I remember one sketch we did. I was the host of a male beauty contest in dinner jacket and bow tie. Benny, the first contestant, came on in a pair of lycra shorts. "This is our first contestant," I said. "Ivor Biggin from Mill Hill."

"No," said Benny. "I'm Ivor Mill from Biggin Hill."

I dated a couple of girls from the series who both told me how they got the jobs. Normally artists would be chosen by the producer or casting director. In Benny's case, he liked to pick the girls himself. He'd see a picture of a girl on page 3 of the *Sun*, ring the photographer Beverley Goodway and ask for their number. Naturally, the girls were interested in progressing into television, so they accepted Benny's invitation to lunch at his flat overlooking Hyde Park. There he'd lay on a light salad lunch, they'd share a bottle of wine and then he'd say, "Let's play a little game. I'll go and hide somewhere in the flat, give it a couple of minutes and then see if you can find me. If you do, you can do what you like with me." This gave the girls a couple of minutes to think, "Is this how you get into television?" Two minutes later they'd find Benny – surprise, surprise – in the bedroom where they pleasured him in the expected manner. Clever Benny. No pregnancies, no angry mothers. No wonder he had that cheeky glint in his eyes as he looked around the studio and surveyed the girls who had successfully passed the audition.

It was political correctness that ended Benny's career – sad for Thames, because his shows earned them millions of pounds around the world.

Via a friend, Rod Harrod, I met a very pretty girl called Angela Downing (nowadays married to a famous pop star), who recommended a friend from her home town, Norwich, Judy Pointer, who she said would make a marvellous personal assistant for me. She was absolutely right. While I was out doing the shows and the gigs, Judy ran the office from the Hallam Street flat. Everyone who wrote for a signed picture got one. Every query about music was answered. I had learned from Ken Dodd the value of good relations with the listening and watching public. Judy made my travel arrangements and booked my hotel accommodation. Because the flat was so near the BBC, record company pluggers dropped off their wares with suggestions of what might be 'Hamilton Hotshots'. When I couldn't get to pop concerts, Judy went on my behalf and reported back so I could talk about them on the air. I always knew with the record pluggers that they were fair-weather friends. They'd entertain you royally at lunch, if you wanted to go, but if you lost your show you wouldn't see them for dust. They, and the recording artists as well, saw Radio 1 purely as a shop window for their material. If they could get close to the DJs or producers, they thought they would get preferential treatment. We got virtually all the records and lots of bottles of booze at Christmas. I was too busy for all the lunches, and my show was at the wrong time, but one producer based at the BBC's Egton House lunched with pluggers so frequently he was nicknamed 'Egton Ronay'.

Judy enjoyed her job so much that she stayed working for me for 30 years, during which time we never had a bad word. That's fairly unique, I'd have thought. A friend of mine, Patrick Stafford, came to do some decorating one day. There must have been something about his lithe body up the ladder, or maybe it was his brush strokes, but Judy became Mrs Patrick Stafford, and I was their best man.

One year for my birthday Judy gave me a book called *Million Selling Records*. It gave me the material for a long-running radio series that I have sold to many radio stations in the UK as well as Spain and Thailand. It was a birthday present that turned out to be worth thousands of pounds, the best present I could have.

There was one girl who kept turning up at beauty contests I hosted, and she kept winning. Her name was Kathy McKinnon and she wasn't a typical beauty contestant. She was small, very pretty but also very bright. After one show she said to me, "You're a very slow worker. When are you going to invite me out?"

I took her up on her offer, we embarked on a torrid affair and in no time she moved in with me at the flat in Hallam Street. Her father was a High Court judge and when he handled a controversial case the press had a

With Kathy McKinnon

field day. They had the lot – the DJ, the Page 3 girl and the judge.

Kathy and I became a very high-profile couple. When we went on holiday to Portugal we were snapped at the airport. We went to the launch of *Abba the Movie* and got more publicity than Abba. Magazines wanted Kathy's beauty tips and my keep fit tips. It wasn't all great, of course. John Junor wrote in the *Sunday Express* – then a huge circulation newspaper – "Does she think the pinnacle of her career is posing topless and titillating in the *Sun* and shacking up with a third-rate disc jockey?" Kathy asked her father if I should sue them. "Definitely," said the judge, no fan of the press. "The words 'third-rate' could be damaging to David's career."

"Are you sure he has a case?" asked Kathy.

"If I don't know, who does?" said Judge McKinnon. So I sued the *Express*. John Junor's defence was that all disc jockeys were third rate per se. We settled out of court. I wasn't looking for money but an apology. Junor refused to apologise but agreed to publish three favourable pictures and stories of Kathy and me within the next year and to pay my solicitors' fees. I'm sure the paper had a fund for that. He was often rude about people.

Time to meet the judge so he could pass judgement on whether my intentions to his daughter were honourable. My visit to the McKinnon home in Purley was made easier by the fact that his wife was a fan of my programme. Judge Neil McKinnon turned out to be an excellent host and a funny storyteller with a fund of jokes about the judiciary. He loved stories about judges who were out of touch with reality. There was the story of a man who was accused of exposing himself on the upper deck of a London bus. "With respect, Your Honour, I feel you may be unfamiliar with the circumstances," said the defence counsel.

"Then I shall make it my business to familiarise myself with them and shall go home this evening on an omnibus," said the judge. That evening he boarded a bus and went upstairs.

"Fares please. Where to?" asked the conductor, to which the judge replied, "Take me to number 13 Beauchamp Place."

Another story concerned an old lag who had been frequently in court for offences involving over use of alcohol. "This is not the first time you have appeared in my courtroom for this kind of offence," said the judge. "In your own interest I am going to send you to prison for six weeks. During this time you will have no access to alcohol whatever." (Wagging his finger:) "Not even a glass of sherry before dinner."

He also told the story of the hangman who was about to hang a woman prisoner. As she walked into the execution room, the hangman said, "You've got a fine figure."

"It's all yours," said the woman. "If you keep your trap shut."

If Kathy and I were to get married, which was the intention, there was first the business of my divorce. I didn't want to make the same mistakes I made with Roz of prevarication and indecision. I asked Sheila for a divorce and reluctantly she agreed. It was also agreed that I would give her the house at Oxshott and that I would continue to pay all the bills and for the children's education. At the age of 37, I said goodbye to everything I had earned in the last 20 years. I was going to have to work extremely hard to pull myself back up again.

CHAPTER 12

Top of the Pops

AFTER my work with Ken Dodd and Benny Hill, Thames put me together with another of our favourite funnymen, Tommy Cooper. The plan was that I would interview him at the end of every show in a six-week series of *Cooper* on ITV in a sketch called 'Fez to Fez'. When I got together with the producer Royston Mayoh he said to me, "I don't want you to be one of those interviewers who falls about with laughter all the time. It'll be much funnier if you play it straight."

When I got the scripts I didn't think there was much danger of falling about. Kathy helped me to learn my lines by reading Tommy's to me at our flat in Hallam Street.

"Do you find this funny?" I asked her. (And, by the way, Kathy had a great sense of humour.)

"I didn't find it funny at all," she said. "I think he's going to die on his arse."

And yet when Tommy said the lines that looked so unfunny on paper, people really did fall about. He was just a naturally funny man. He was funny-looking for a start. My theory is that he could have read the phone directory and people would have found it hilarious.

The series was recorded at the Thames studios by the river at Teddington where so many of their best shows were done. (Now, sadly, a block of flats.) We rehearsed in an upstairs room at The Anglers pub next door to the studios. For Tommy this was lethal. He was a heavy drinker and all-day trays of drinks were brought up to the rehearsal room. One evening he had so much to drink they had to send the audience home, posting a notice saying 'Unfortunately, Tommy Cooper Is Indisposed. Your Tickets Will Be Valid For Another Date'. Indisposed he certainly was. Losing a studio day was an expensive business, but Tommy was still commanding big ratings. "Once, Tommy," the studio bosses told him, "but never again." It never happened again.

When we got to the studio, Tommy never stuck to the script. There was a great deal of ad-libbing. "What's this?" I said to myself, frantically thinking how I could get him back on course towards the tag line at the end of the sketch. With Lyndsey De Paul providing the musical highlights, *Cooper* went out on a weekday evening at 8 o'clock and was a moderate ratings success, though by this time drink was beginning to dominate his life. Nine years later, at the age of just 63, he died on stage during the show *Live at Her Majesty's*. Everyone thought his collapse was a gag. He went out to a full house and lots of laughter. Just the way Tommy would have liked it.

While I was enjoying my time with the comics, Delia, my stepmother, had moved from her council flat in Gap Road to another flat on the edge of Wimbledon Common. As my father died penniless and she was long retired, it occurred to me that she might be short of money. As I was now doing well, I could afford to help her out. One day, dressed in a flowery shirt on the way to the radio studio, I popped round to her flat with an envelope full of cash to give her. As she opened the door, I was confronted by her and her three sisters all dressed in black and looking at me incredulously. It turned out that Percy, her brother, had died and they were getting ready to go to his funeral. I apologised for my incredibly bad timing and inappropriate clothing, left the envelope on the table and swiftly left. It was only later that I pondered why nobody had told me that Percy had died or invited me to the funeral. The outsider, as ever.

In 1975, the year I worked with Tommy Cooper, the BBC was having one of its periodical economy cuts, when it was decided to axe the afternoon show on Radio 2 and for my show to be heard on both Radio 1 and Radio 2. Radio 2 at the time had an enormously powerful signal and could be heard from the west of Ireland to Paris. Being on the two networks gave the show a huge audience, the biggest of the day. The show remained exactly the same. No concessions were made to the Radio 2 audience. It was still a Radio 1 show that they happened to take.

As a Radio 1 DJ, the one gig missing from my schedule was *Top of the Pops*. Thames wouldn't let me do it while I was working for them, and *Top of the Pops* wouldn't have me on their rota if I was appearing on Thames. It was such a big show at the time that families would sit round the television on Thursday nights speculating about what might be number 1 that week. DJ-ing was now such a big part of my life that I felt I really ought to be doing it. It was a huge decision to leave Thames because they had been so good to me and my announcing work led to so many shows, but my mind was made up. In January 1976, I gave up my job at Thames for a once-a-month slot on *Top of the Pops*, with the promise that the BBC would come up with other shows for me to do. I was part of a team that comprised, mainly, Noel Edmonds, Tony Blackburn and Jimmy Savile. Savile was much older than the other hosts but, as a producer said to me, "We could never get rid of Jimmy Savile. He's an institution." How, I wondered, do you become an institution?

Radio 1 football team

The first time I stepped into the *Top of the Pops* studio at BBC Television Centre in White City I was surprised at how small it was. With clever direction it looked much bigger, but in fact there were about a hundred teenagers who the floor manager shunted from one set to another. One minute they were watching David Essex on one set, the next they were herded across to see Rod Stewart on another. The other shock was the fee. *Top of the Pops* was a very cheap show to produce. Most of the bands and singers appeared for nothing, as an appearance on the show almost guaranteed their record would climb up the chart. They were queuing up, some almost begging, to be on there. In those days, the BBC was very careful with its money. Unlike today when presenters like Gary Lineker are paid astronomical sums, *Top of the Pops* hosts were poorly paid. My fee was £75 – for a show attracting 15 million viewers. It was recorded on a Wednesday evening and transmitted the following night. After the recording I would do a disco in The Dun Cow pub in the Old Kent Road (nowadays a dental surgery) where Kenny Scott, the owner, paid me £300 for working to 200 customers. The TV and radio shows gave us the shop window for the gigs which we had to do to make some decent money.

By the mid-'70s *Top of the Pops* had become like a conveyor belt, with a blasé crew churning out show after show. Every ITV studio I had worked in had been fun with lots of banter between the artists and the crew through the day. It was a hoot, a joy to go to work, though always businesslike when it came to the output. At the start of a *Top of the Pops* I said to the floor manager, "Do something funny to make me laugh."

"You do it," he said. "You're a professional." Ouch.

True to their word, the BBC did come up with more shows for me. Along with other Radio 1 DJs I was one of the hosts of *Seaside Special*, the show that toured Britain's resorts and occupied the Saturday night light entertainment slot on BBC 1. What fun the shows were, recorded under Gerry Cottle's circus tent. My favourites were at the end of the summer when, blessed with glorious weather, we filmed in Guernsey, then on the ferry to Jersey and then did two shows in the capital St Helier. Mid-'70s music was happy, the comics made us laugh and the dancers added youth and energy.

I was also a frequent panellist of *Blankety Blank*, the show that depended so much on Terry Wogan's warmth and sparkling wit. Unlike so many TV shows, nothing was ever planned. Terry just made it up as he went along, and it was all the better for that. It drew huge audiences. Whereas today contestants win big money, the prizes were a *Blankety Blank* chequebook and pen.

I always looked forward to the Radio 1 Roadshows – out of the studio for a week and off on a tour of the seaside resorts. Crowds of 5,000 on a beach watched nothing more than a guy playing records and a few silly games like 'Bits and Pieces' and 'Spot the Mileage' with Smiley Miley. They were all great fun, except the one at Margate when I got pelted with hard boiled eggs and was told, "That's for what you said about Teddy Boys." I can't remember ever mentioning them. Wrong DJ, wrong station, probably.

Then there was the Radio 1 Road Show that I hosted with Annie Nightingale at Mallory Park. Among the guests were the Bay City Rollers. It was the height of Rollermania, as I realised when I introduced them on

The Radio 1 Road Show

stage on their UK tour. At Mallory Park they jumped onto a boat on a lake to get away from their female fans. The fans jumped in fully-clothed and swam out after them. It was the biggest fan frenzy I'd seen since I introduced David Cassidy on his UK tour. He hated the fans screaming so he put cotton wool in his ears. Then, unfortunately, he couldn't hear the band. While he was here, he would have loved to have gone horse riding and seen the countryside. Instead, he spent all his time holed up in his hotel room, hiding from the fans. Even then they shinned up the drainpipe trying to get at him.

People in Ireland were starved of pop music and now they were receiving my Radio 1 show (via Radio 2) I started getting requests to appear at discos over there. An agent called Arthur Walters, based in Dublin, offered to get me some gigs in the Emerald Isle and, since my father was born in Dublin, I was keen to see his home country. My first gig was in Thurles, and I discovered it really is a long way to Tipperary. The shows in Ireland all started late, drink flowed and, as the Irish say, there was good *craic*.

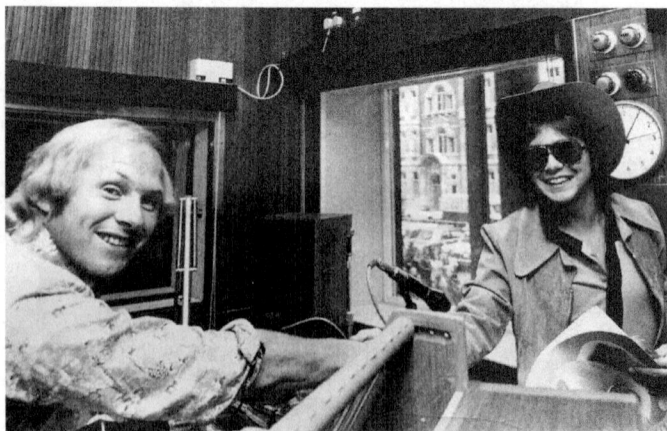

In Radio 1 studio with David Cassidy

After a while Arthur suggested we venture north of the border. It was the time of the Troubles and I was the first BBC DJ to have visited there in a long time. Kid Jensen had been there, but he's Canadian. Rosko had been, but he's American. I was the first English one to go. I have to say there were lots of times I was nervous. Arthur had Southern Ireland number plates and often in the pitch black of night we'd be stopped on the road by a blinding white light. Might it be the paramilitaries?, I wondered. No, fortunately, it was the Garda, the Irish police, checking who we were. Before I went on stage at a hotel in Londonderry, the owner said to me, "I'm very proud of this hotel. It's the only one in the city that hasn't been blown up yet." It was the way he said yet that bothered me. It was at that hotel that I found the crowd shouting at me when I said, "It's great to be here in Londonderry tonight."

"What are they shouting?" I asked Arthur.

"Derry," he said. "They like to call it Derry."

I learnt as I went along. Often the punters told me what they wanted me to play. One evening a man said in my ear, "Provos rule."

"I haven't got that," I said. "Would The Undertones do?" Ignorance is bliss.

We were on the road in Ireland the weekend Lord Mountbatten was killed at Mullaghmore. Heading North from Dublin, we heard the shocking news on Arthur's car radio. It was the same weekend that 18 British soldiers were killed at Warrenpoint. I was due on stage that evening at Bangor. I don't think I played any records. No one was in the mood for dancing.

I did lots of weekends on the road in Ireland. Sometimes I'd do a double (two gigs on the same night in different towns) on Friday and Saturday, then a show

141

on Sunday night, followed by a drive to Dublin and, without going to bed, catch the first flight from Dublin to London on Monday, getting back in time to check in to the flat and get ready for the show on Radio 1. One such Monday a large envelope arrived and I recognised Sheila's handwriting. It contained a pile of bills to pay which wiped out everything I'd just earned over the weekend. The price of running two homes. No one to blame but myself.

With Kathy McKinnon

Meanwhile, life with Kathy was always fun. Not only was her father a judge, but her two brothers were barristers and later became judges. She rebelled against her legal background, not only in her work but in her private life as well. There was a strong lobby to legalise cannabis and she would have gladly signed the petition in *The Times* to make that happen. She wore a small bag around

her neck that she called her dope bag. It contained cigarette papers and pieces of hash. One day she couldn't
find her dope bag in the flat and she, Judy and I started
searching frantically through waste paper baskets and
other nooks and crannies that it might have fallen into.
When we drew a blank, I said, "Let's think about what
might have left the flat."

"The laundry was collected today," said Judy. So

*As the 'Housewives' Superstar', according
to the* Sunday Telegraph *magazine*

she phoned the laundry in Wimbledon and asked, "Has Mr. Hamilton's laundry arrived from Hallam Street? If so, I think there might be a bag with some valuables in it."

The man who answered the call said, "Let me go and have a look." He came back a couple of minutes later and said, "Yes, it is here. There is a bag, but no valuables. Just some cigarette papers and what looks like some... grass." I think he meant grass, as in lawn.

"We'll send a taxi over right away to pick it up," said Judy. Radio DJs were being busted for less at the time. If the man had known what it was he could have made a few quid out of selling the story to the press.

Kathy was keen for me to join her in her smoking habit. I'd never smoked cigarettes or taken any drugs. "You're so square," she said. So I tried it. It didn't have any great effect on me apart from a craving for Mars Bars and a wish to lie down, but it did get me hooked on nicotine and I became a cigarette smoker, something perhaps unwise given that both my parents had died young of lung cancer. It was a habit that took me some time to get rid of, and then that happened dramatically.

Kathy was also an exhibitionist. She had a wonderful body and was not shy of sharing it with others in newspapers and magazines. At a party she took all her clothes off and danced on a table. I have to say the thought crossed my mind of how I would feel if she did this when she was Mrs Hamilton.

CHAPTER 13

To America

I was known as 'One-Take Hamilton'. I did everything in one take. But one day my reputation took a bashing. Standing on a dais on the *Top of the Pops* set, getting ready to introduce Rod Stewart singing 'The Killing of Georgie', I found myself saying, "And now Rod Stewart and 'The Killing of Georgie Fame'."

"Cut," yelled the floor manager, looking up at me. "It's not Georgie Fame."

"I know," I said, feeling foolish.

"OK, let's go for another take," said the floor manager. I know how annoying that was for the director and crew because they liked to record *Top of the Pops*, as live – in other words, in one go.

"Stand by, studio – and cue David," said the FM.

Off I went again. "And now Rod Stewart and 'The Killing of Georgie Fame'."

I found people looking at me very strangely and hushed discussions going on between the floor manager and the director. As I stood there on the dais I had a very strange feeling. I just didn't feel myself. I felt as though I was in a bad dream.

Months later, I was talking to a couple of guys from a record company. One of them said, "Do you remember when you introduced Rod Stewart singing Georgie Fame? Well, we slipped something in your drink in the BBC canteen before the show." Bearing in mind my principle of never drinking alcohol before a show, they must have spiked my tea or water.

"And you thought that was funny?" I asked.

"Yes, it was hilarious," they said.

I know that pranks did go on – and I did some of them – but on this occasion I lost my sense of humour. The bookings for *Top of the Pops* dried up. I was no longer Mr Reliable. Since I'd left Thames so that I could do *TOTP*, I wondered if I should go back. When I asked, they welcomed me back with open arms. They even asked me to join them on a trip to New York to sell Thames programmes to the American market. For five days, Monday to Friday, Thames took over WOR TV, Channel 9, in New York. In a swap arrangement between Thames and WOR, Dick Cavett came to London to host some chat shows and Eamonn Andrews went to New York to do the same. I did the continuity announcing, as in London, mainly in vision and read the evening news for New Yorkers.

When I rocked up at the WOR studios in Times Square in the centre of New York on the first day, I was introduced to the WOR gang in the offices. One I got chatting to was a woman researcher, laid off for the week as Thames were in town.

"As you guys are here, I'm writing a book. Would you like to see some?" I started reading her prose: it was so explicit and erotic that it came as quite a shock. "Drop by tomorrow for chapter 2," she said.

So each day I dropped by for a further chapter and it just got hotter and hotter. I thought of things I might say to her, like, "Anyone who could write this stuff must be…" but everything seemed so corny so I kept my opinions to myself.

The week went extremely well, Thames sold lots of

programmes to America and on the last night they threw a party in the big studio. I stayed in my announcer's studio. I had recorded the links for the night but I had to be there in case of a breakdown. Halfway through the evening I had a visit from the randy researcher. "You look very lonely," she said.

"Yes, I feel like Cinderella."

"Can I get you a glass of wine?"

For once I broke my golden rule of not drinking before or during work. What the hell, I thought. The week has been a great success and the chances were I had nothing more to do.. None of the bosses were watching. They were all at the party. So we enjoyed a glass of wine together. She then offered me a funny cigarette.

"Here in the studio?" I asked.

"Everybody does it here," she said.

So we had a little smoke. "Is there anything else I can do for you?" she asked.

We walked down the corridor to the number 1 dressing room. It was the only one that had a bed. Silly not to make the most of it. While we were *in flagrante delicto*, I fancied I heard the door open gently and then close again. I discovered later that it was Eamonn Andrews' dressing room and he'd popped back to pick something up. I was also told that Eamonn, who was a little straightlaced, not to say puritanical, had said, "That man will never appear on *This Is Your Life*." I never did. Until Michael Aspel took over.

The following morning I went round to Marion's apartment to say a passionate goodbye. Her car was parked outside. The number plate read NO MERCY.

Despite my indiscretion, two years later Thames took me on another trip to the USA, this time to KHJ Channel 9 in Los Angeles and with a bigger line up – Eamonn

Andrews (again), Ernie Wise (Eric Morecambe was unwell and couldn't make it) and the distinguished newsreader Andrew Gardner. And this time my role was increased. At 11 am I would co-host *Mid-Morning LA* with the regular American host, I'd do the continuity announcing and in the evening I would co-anchor the News At Ten with Andrew Gardner. I had read news on local TV in England but I found it daunting sharing the duties with such a master of his craft.

There was a lot of interest in LA about our visit. When I spoke to the press, I told them that back home I was a disc jockey. What was I thinking of? In the land of film stars DJs were ten a penny. That's surely why Emperor Rosko came to Britain.

On the first night at KHJ the bulletin was set. Andrew and I had run through it on autocue and were ready to go. At 9.30 the news came through that John Wayne had died. The whole bulletin had to be re-set and we went on air live at 10 without having read the autocue. Andrew launched the bulletin with, "The Duke is dead." The LA press complimented our measured delivery and our understanding of Stateside culture.

The *Hollywood Reporter* described us as newsmen of the Walter Cronkite School, in a flattering reference to the great American anchor.

The week went so well and Thames sold so many shows to the West Coast market that Brian Cowgill, the MD, told us, "As a little Thank-You we're taking you to Las Vegas for the weekend." No one argued. So we hopped on a flight to Vegas and booked into the Sands hotel. I'd never seen anything like it. There were slot machines everywhere, even in the loos. The windows were bolted in case anyone decided to jump off – publicity they could do without. On the Saturday night we saw

Hallelujah Hollywood, the most spectacular show I've ever seen, hosted by Gene Kelly. There were topless dancers with feather headdresses, a hilarious act featuring orangutans and other acts on wires flying in above our heads from all angles.

The following night it was Dean Martin at the MGM Grand. Dean came out to rapturous applause and did a little dance routine with a drink in his hand, after which he said, "Who's the mother who says it's the legs that go first?" Behind him was the biggest orchestra I've

Eamonn Andrews, DH, Brian Cowgill, MD of Thames Television, Ernie Wise and Andrew Gardner.

ever seen. Must have been 40-piece. Dean looked at the orchestra and then asked the audience, "What are these people doing in my bedroom?"

"He doesn't drink," said Ernie Wise who was sitting next to me.

"You don't think so?" I asked.

"No one could have that perfect timing if they were drunk," said Ernie. And if anyone knew about perfect timing it was Ernie Wise.

A few days later, I was back home opening the Miners' Gala in Grimethorpe. Down to earth with a bang.

CHAPTER 14

To Radio 2

B Y the mid-'70s all the hard work of the last 15 years was starting to pay off. I was hardly an overnight sensation but after a steady climb I had got to the place where I aimed to be. I had a daily show on Radio 1 and Radio 2. I was doing plenty of television. Warwick Records released a compilation album of 'Hamilton's Hotshots' which reached the Top 20 of the album chart at a time when compilation albums were still allowed in the charts. On stage I did my third pantomime, topping the bill in *Aladdin* at the New Victoria Theatre in London. It was one of Bill Kenwright's first productions

Aladdin, New Victoria Theatre, London, 1976

and I was part of a double act with Kenneth Connor from the 'Carry On' films: Kenny Quickbrew and Diddy David Typhoo, two Chinese 'tea leaves'. Bill agreed to delay the matinee time so I could dash there in time from my radio show. Among those in the audience on the opening night was my beautiful girlfriend, Kathy McKinnon. We were always plastered over the newspapers. We joked that we only had to fart and it made news. The *Sunday Telegraph* put me on the cover of its Sunday magazine with the caption 'Housewives' Superstar'. Among the pictures inside was one of me with my Rolls Royce.

Sadly, the Rolls was the subject of much vandalism, even though I didn't have a personalised plate. When I left a concert by the wonderful American band, Bread, at the New Victoria Theatre, I discovered that someone had been round it with a nail file and left a deep scratch in every panel, including the boot and the bonnet. Another time someone threw nail polish all over the boot. The Flying Lady, the Spirit of Ecstasy – the iconic mascot on a Rolls Royce bonnet – was stolen five times. Eventually, I had it wired to the horn. Once in a restaurant I heard the horn blaring and saw a man leap into the air and then run off. Certainly in the '70s a Rolls was a car you could garage at home and drive it to someone else's house where they had a garage. Left anywhere else, it was a target of envy and anger.

On the plus side, I was voted one of the best dressed men on television, one of the top tie men and second to Des O'Connor as owner of the best television smile. Not a day went by without a request to open something or appear somewhere. Woman magazine readers voted me number 2 as the 'Biggest TV Turn-On' after Tom Selleck, the 6ft 4 star of the hit detective show *Magnum, P.I.* My quote was, "If he's a Magnum, I must be a Babycham."

I was able to pick and choose my gigs more carefully. Instead of Plymouth tonight, Aberdeen tomorrow I was able to do three nights in neighbouring towns and cities – say, Manchester, Liverpool and Bolton. And I added a go-go dancer to my act. When appearing at Ragamuffin's Club in Camberley, I was approached by a girl who asked if she could dance on stage. I told her I didn't use dancers in my act. "You will when you see me," she said. She was so persuasive that I let her go ahead. She was sensational. The audience loved her. She told me afterwards that she was an African princess, and naturally I believed her.

I started to use 'Princess Balou' more and more. In her act she invited a male member of the audience up on stage to dance with her and pretended to undress him. One night at a club in Essex, emboldened by a certain amount of wacky-baccy, she did actually remove a man's clothes. Some women protested to the club owner, who announced that he would never have the Princess or me back at the club again. Someone leaked the story to the *News of the World*, which ran it with the headline: 'DIDDY DAVID DISCO DANCER BANNED'. The following day the phone rang off the hook with offers to me of appearances in clubs, all insisting I bring my dancer with me. All good publicity for my Radio 1 show.

One man who possibly didn't see it that way was the Controller of Radio 1, Derek Chinnery. In 1977, he called me into his office and told me that the BBC now had the money to separate the networks in the afternoon and that later that year I would be moving to Radio 2. He made it sound like a kind of demotion, and that was how I saw it: Radio 1 was the place I had always wanted to be, whereas Radio 2 was very much a middle of the road station. Why was he prepared to let me go when my show was doing so well? In time I pressed him for an answer. "Basically, it's a matter of age," he said. Since I was still in my thirties and he was several years older and wore a pinstripe suit, I thought that was rich. Also at a party he threw at his home in Hampstead I noticed from his LP collection that the choice of home listening of the Controller of Radio 1 were the 1950s musicals *South Pacific* and *The Sound of Music*.

Stories about Chinnery abounded. When Lou Reed's record 'Walk on the Wild Side' was released, Chinnery wondered if, in view of changing public opinion, the BBC might this time play it. "I will listen to the lyrics," he said. "And to hear them clearly, I will play the record at a slower speed." When it came to the line about giving head, he said, "Presumably a reference to buggery."

"Not surprising," said one of his assistants. "He's been talking through his arse for years."

On another occasion he asked one of the DJs what he did in his spare time. The DJ told him he played a lot of pool. "Ah, swimming. Very good for you," said Chinnery.

By the autumn of '77 this true man of the people told me that my move to Radio 2 would happen in November. On the day of my last programme he sat opposite me in the studio – something he had never done before – presumably to dissuade me from mentioning that I would be moving to Radio 2. It worked.

My last record was Neil Sedaka and 'Our Last Song Together'. It all sounded very final. With the show over, he carried my jingles out to my car. How considerate. That was all the thanks I got for all the big audiences I had got them over a period of time. Looking back, I suppose I was lucky that I was moving to Radio 2. Many DJs in the future wouldn't have that luxury. As we would see in times to come, the BBC would have a track record of knifing its stars in the back.

Chinnery's master plan was to move Tony Blackburn from the morning and put him in direct competition with me in the afternoon. Blackburn and I had had a friendly rivalry on air at Radio 1, a way of cross-promoting each other's shows. Now we were up against each other. For

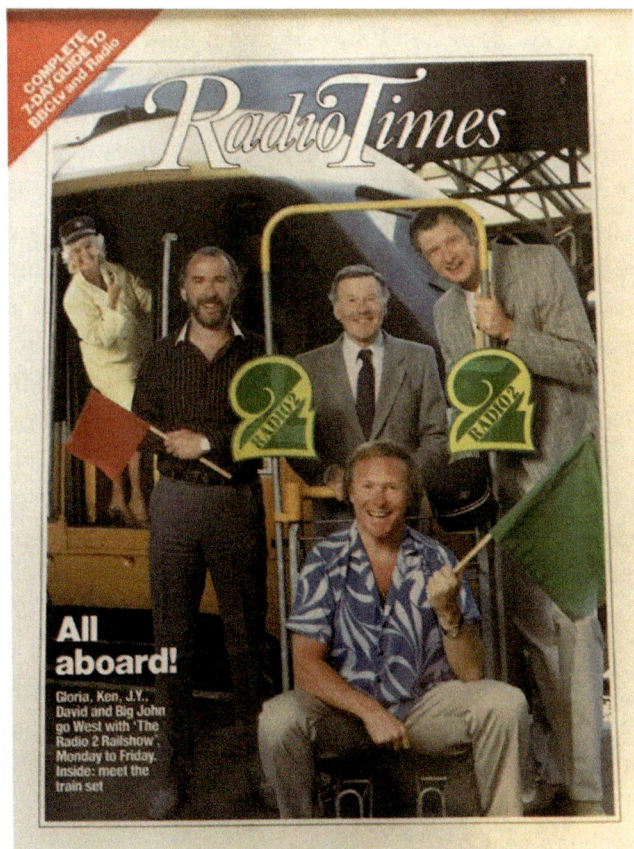

Radio 2 DJs Gloria Hunniford, Ken Bruce,
Jimmy Young, John Dunn and DH

some reason his show started a week before mine, a trick missed by Radio 2.

Hardly had my show been on air than Paul Williams, my former producer and now Blackburn's, came bursting into my studio, screaming: "You're playing our music!" Since it was Abba on the turntable I couldn't understand what he was talking about. I didn't know Radio 1 had them under exclusive contract. Chinnery leaned on Geoff Owen, head of Radio 2, to remove any semblance of pop music from my show. Owen resisted, saying, "You worry about your music and I'll worry about mine."

When it was clear that I was moving to Radio 2, the first thing they did was despatch me to Sandown Park to meet ace horse racing commentator Peter Bromley. I sat next to Peter in his commentary box and marvelled at his art of identifying the horses as they raced around the circuit. Over the next few years, horse racing would become the bane of my life. Radio 2 covered all the big meetings, and some of the smaller ones. When I was doing the shared show across two networks I wouldn't have known they were there. The Radio 1 show carried on as normal. Once the show was originated by Radio 2, I'd have to fade a record halfway through because a sports producer on the talkback from the control room next door was telling me that Peter Bromley was bellowing at him for me to handover to the racing. Very often there was then about five minutes' waffle while the horses were being loaded into the stalls before the race finally got underway. It became a tug of war between music and sport. By no means were all music lovers interested in horse racing. Equally, I understood, not all racing fans wanted to hear music.

It wasn't just racing. For two weeks, every summer my show was replaced by coverage of Wimbledon Tennis, though most people watched it on television. By the time Steve Wright became the afternoon man some years later, sport had moved to a new home, Radio 5, where it was uninterrupted by a man wanting to play his records.

A Song For Europe with Ken Bruce and Terry Wogan

There were problems with the music, too. There were two factions within Radio 2. In one camp were the David Jacobs, 'Our Kind of Music' clan, who wanted to play standards and big band music. In the other were younger producers who wanted the pop music of the day, though obviously not punk or heavy metal.

Luckily, Geoff Owen let these producers loose on my show and in my time at Radio 2 I had three very good producers who I worked harmoniously with – Martin Cox, Chris Vezey and Geoff Mullin.

Despite all the interruptions from the horse racing and other sport, we more than held our own against Radio 1.

In fact, it wasn't too long before Tony Blackburn was moved off to Junior Choice at the weekends.

With the wonderful Gene Pitney

One very popular feature of the show was 'The Music Game' (a forerunner of Ken Bruce's 'Popmaster'), where contestants would win LPs for answering questions on music. The most successful ones went forward to a final in front of an audience in the Concert Hall in Broadcasting House. This was hotly contested, with some real musical eggheads. Alan Jarvie from East Kilbride, who won it in 1986, remains a good friend and is now presenting radio shows in Scotland

I would stay nine years at Radio 2, twice as long as my time at Radio 1. It would have been longer had it not been for a Controller who took the station in a completely wrong direction: one I could not pursue.

CHAPTER 15

To Fulham

I'D never thought of being a director of a football club but when the idea was mooted I quite fancied it – the chance to be involved with the running of the club I'd supported all my life, barring a short defection to Charlton during the Sam Bartram era.

It came about through a set of unusual events. In 1975, Fulham had one of their most glorious days – a Cup Final at Wembley – and they got there the hard way, by winning all their matches away from home. Along with my son, David junior, and some friends, our travels took in Sheffield and Carlisle on the way to Wembley. A problem arose with the semi-final replay against Birmingham City at Maine Road, Manchester. I was on the air at Radio 1 until five o'clock; kick-off in Manchester was at 7.45. There was no scheduled flight or train that could get me there in time, and I certainly wouldn't do it by car. Six of us hired a Piper Aztec to take us from Northolt to Ringway, where my old pal and Manchester City director Freddie Pye picked us up in his Roller and whisked us to Maine Road. We were in the ground ten minutes after kick-off, in good time to see John Mitchell's late goal take us to Wembley.

Sadly, after being brilliant through all the rounds, Fulham, despite having Bobby Moore in the side against his old club West Ham, froze on the big day. A shot from

Alan Taylor went right through our goalkeeper Peter Mellor's legs.

"I'm sorry, boss," said Peter to the manager Alec Stock in the dressing room after the game. "I should have kept my legs closed."

Alec Stock replied dryly, "Your mother should have done that years ago."

Not long after the Wembley fiasco, Fulham's chairman, the veteran comedian Tommy Trinder ("You lucky people") was ousted in a boardroom coup. The man who replaced him was a blunt Yorkshireman with a thick neck and a crewcut called Ernie Clay. Clay's roots were in Rugby League, which he introduced at Craven Cottage with some success over a limited time, though it carved up the pitch and made it difficult to play soccer on.

There was tragedy at Fulham when one of the directors, Sir Eric Miller, chairman of Peachy Property and knighted by Harold Wilson in his resignation honours list, committed suicide by putting two bullets through his brain, quite a difficult thing to do. He had been the subject of a fraud squad enquiry.

Ernie Clay was now looking for people to invest in the club. One man he approached was Edward Burston, a wealthy businessman, who sat high up in the Riverside Stand at matches with his attractive Japanese girlfriend, Emiko. Burston wanted to help the club but had no trust in Clay and suspected his plan was to sell the ground, which was on a prime site next to the Thames, for development. Edward Burston was a Fulham fanatic and would frequently invite me to his apartment overlooking Hyde Park, where he would show me videos of Fulham's matches. On every visit he would give me a Fulham shirt. Eventually I had enough shirts for an entire team. Over dinner one evening he expressed to me his concerns about Clay. "What we need on the board are genuine Fulham supporters, not businessmen who see the ground as a crock of gold. People like you," he said. He went on to say that Clay's condition of anybody joining was that they would lend the club £25,000. I explained that, having just gone through an expensive divorce, I didn't have that kind of money but I could try to raise funds for the club by doing events like discos for them. Edward conveyed this message to Ernie Clay and said that he would join the board as a director only if I joined as well under the conditions I had outlined.

Thus in July 1978, I joined the board of directors at Fulham FC, buying, as agreed with Clay, 100 £1 shares. I was told the code of behaviour in the directors' box: no jumping up and down when the team score, being courteous to directors of the opposing club and being magnanimous in victory. I started going to all the matches, home and away. On the away trips I paid my own travel expenses. There was no question of the club paying them, even though I was there on duty.

Sitting next to Ernie Clay in the directors' box, it was pretty clear he didn't know much about football. In a match at Queen's Park Rangers one of their players, Tony Currie, scored with a rocket shot from at least 25 yards out. "That's class," I said to Clay.

"Could have gone anywhere in the ground," he said.

Well, it didn't. It went right into the back of the net. When I told Tony Currie this story some years later he thought it was hilarious.

Not all of being a football director was grim. I'd become good friends with Les Strong, the captain of the promotion winning team in 1982.

"You've become a bit stick up," he said. "We don't see much of you these days."

"Clay told me now I was a director not to fraternise with the players."

"Stuff him," said Strongey. "We're your mates."

I took his advice and had a drink with him at the bar after a Noon Saturday kick-off at Crystal Palace.

"As it happens, Les, you had a good game."

"Funny you should say that", he replied. "Last night Bestey and I were out on the piss, we didn't go to bed at all and to be honest we were still pissed when we kicked off at 12 o'clock."

I said, "My advice to you as a director of the club is this. If you can play like that on a Saturday afternoon, make that your regular training schedule on a Friday night."

Fulham and Chelsea were great fun places to be in the '70 and '80s. There were wonderful restaurants and you could park virtually outside the door. One we frequented was the Casserole in the Kings Road. The French food was delicious and in the background was always fabulous music. It was there for the first time that I heard Don McLean's 'American Pie', one of the best records ever made. "Wow, what is this?" we all said.

Just off the Kings Road was The Gasworks, a quirky establishment whose clientele ranged from villains to coppers, Princess Margaret and John Bindon. It was run by an eccentric couple called Jack and Shirley. Jack was rude to all the customers and Shirley spent her time in the kitchen cooking with a fag in her mouth. The menu was steak or chicken, the wine list was house white or red. There was a huge chess board whose pieces were figures from the Karma Sutra and there were bawdy photographs in the lavatories. In the air was a heavy smell of marijuana. Everyone I took there loved it.

Further up the Kings Road was another restaurant

whose name escapes me. It had a huge blackboard on a wall and customers were invited to chalk on it witty comments. If the owner thought they weren't that funny, he'd rub them off at the end of the night, but if he liked them they'd stay longer. One message that stayed there for months on end was aimed at the much maligned Roddy Llewellyn. It read...

RODDY LLEWELLYN HAS JUST TAKEN UP ACTING. HE'S GOT A VERY SMALL PART IN CHARLEY'S AUNT.

I did some discos for nothing and raised some money for the club and got some DJ pals to appear at a reduced rate as well. Another recruit to the board was the singer and keyboard player Alan Price, from the band The Animals. I'm not sure if he gave the club any money or raised funds for them with shows but I do know that when we played Sunderland he wore a red and white scarf in the directors' box.

After a while it became clear that none of the directors were going to have any say in the running of the club. It was a dictatorship. When Fulham became the subject of a Football Association enquiry into illegal payments to players, Burston and I asked to see the club's books. Clay refused. We pondered how we could be directors if we couldn't see the state of the club's finances. Working for the BBC, I couldn't afford a scandal so, after just two years on the board, I offered my resignation. Clay asked for the return of my £100 worth of shares. Burston was convinced that Clay was getting hold of as many shares as he could so that he would have control of the club and the ground. So I dug my heels in. "Show me in writing where it says I have to give them back, and I'll do it."

Clay left a message on my answerphone, threatening, "Give those shares back or I could do something that could be harmful to your career." I wasn't aware of any skeletons in the cupboard but I didn't like his tone.

I gave my shares back and that ended my stint as a football club director. What I learned from my time on the board is that the less you know about the running of a football club, the more you can savour it. From this point on I'd be happier watching from the stands, although I did enjoy a working relationship with Fulham some years later.

It was much more fun playing football in charity matches for the Showbiz XI alongside stars like Tommy Steele, Elton John and Rod Stewart. Elton's uncle, Roy Dwight, had played for Fulham and Nottingham Forest, but Rod was definitely the best player in the team. For someone who had dreamed of being a professional footballer, it was wonderful to have the opportunity to play on league grounds and often against recently retired ex-pro footballers. Tony Williams, who was the commentator of the Showbiz XI, took the mickey out of us while we ran up and down doing our best. "At number 7 for the Showbiz XI is David Hamilton. We got him on a free transfer from Subbuteo. No 8 is Robert Powell, who played Jesus of Nazareth. That's why he's no good on crosses." (Ouch.) "Jess Conrad, the goalkeeper, is known as Cinderella because he's always late for the ball."

Jess, the handsome brute, was a good goalie but sometimes dived towards a cameraman's lens rather than the ball. He had a nice line in self-deprecating humour. He said he became a goalkeeper because he fancied the costume. At his 40th wedding anniversary he said, "A lot of people ask what is the secret of Renée and my long-running marriage. It's simple. For 40 years we've both been in love with the same man."

I wore the number 7 shirt for the Showbiz XI for over 20 years, playing my last game at the age of 50. During that time we raised over £3 million for various charities, a lot of money then. In return for my long service, they made me the Honorary President. Margaret Thatcher became our Patron and often sent us 'Good Luck' messages that were printed in match programmes.

One of the most important matches we played was for the dependants of the people who died in the Bradford City fire disaster at their ground, Valley Parade, in May 1985. The match was hurriedly arranged and played at Fartown, the home of Huddersfield Rugby League club. When our coach arrived, people were queuing round the block. It was a sell-out. Our team included Tommy Cannon, of Cannon and Ball, Rick Wakeman, Jeremy

Tony Williams (commentator) with the Showbiz XI playing for the Bradford City fire disaster fund, including Frank Worthington, Tommy Cannon, Rick Wakeman, Jeremy Beadle, Lennie Bennett, Jess Conrad, Tony Selby, Frazer Hines, Jim Dooley, Jim Diamond and stars of Emmerdale and Corrie

Beadle, Tony Selby from *Get Some In*, pop stars Jim Dooley and Jim Diamond as well as stars from *Emmerdale* and *Coronation Street*. We played against an ex-Leeds United XI that included Billy Bremner, Jack Charlton, Johnny Giles and Norman Hunter. Were we mad? When ex-pro Frank Worthington turned up, he insisted on playing for us. "I always wanted to be in show business," he said. No one argued. A real player on our side! (Apparently, Frank's Elvis impersonation was something to behold). Coverage of the match was shown on *News at Ten*.

As well as the Showbiz XI, I played for other teams: the Entertainers XI; the Happy Wanderers, a team of Fulham supporters and ex-players; and I went on a trip to Tampa Bay with the Commentators XI that included John Motson, Martin Tyler, Alan Parry and Jim Rosenthal as well as ex-pros Denis Law, Roger Hunt, Ian St John and Peter Mellor. Radio 1 made me captain of their football team probably because, apart from John Peel, I was the only DJ remotely interested in football. When we played at Sunderland's old ground, Roker Park, we drew

Lining up with the great Bobby Charlton at Old Trafford

the biggest crowd they'd had there all season. Another big crowd turned out to see us play at Old Trafford against an ex-Man U team, boosted no doubt by the appearance on our team of the great Bobby Charlton. Bobby scored direct from a corner kick with his right foot. Somebody said it was a fluke, so in the second half he scored direct from a corner again, this time with his left foot. And this time nobody said it was a fluke.

Nothing beats playing at your own club and I played in several testimonial matches at Fulham and even in a Fulham side in a pre-season friendly. The highlight was in Alan Mullery's testimonial, where the ex-Fulham and England captain had lined up the 1966 World Cup-winning team just ten years after that great triumph to play against an ex-Fulham XI. Mullers called me up at home and said, "I've got the entire World Cup squad bar two who are not available. So rather than get a couple of other pros, I'm asking you and Jimmy Tarbuck if you'd like to play for England." Tarby and I ran out in the famous red and white strip along with the likes of Bobby Moore and Bobby and Jack Charlton. Quite frankly, it doesn't get better than that.

CHAPTER 16

To Barnes and the Arrangement

WE'D had some scorching summers in the '70s and by 1977 I thought it would be nice to have a house with a garden and somewhere to enjoy the sunshine that I always loved. So I put the flat in Hallam Street on the market and Kathy found a house opposite a common in Barnes. The *Daily Mirror* pictured me carrying her over the threshold.

Not long afterwards we were driving somewhere when she told me she wasn't very happy. It came like a bolt out of the blue.

"In fact," she said, "I haven't been happy for a while."

I guess I was too busy to have noticed. She said she would move out but had nowhere to go so I gave her the deposit on a house in Battersea and that enabled her to get on to the property ladder. In our four years together we'd lived our lives in the spotlight – photographed at airports, at opening nights, wherever we went. When news got out that she was leaving, a bunch of photographers were camped outside the house trying to get pictures of her. In fact, she wasn't there but I was indoors with Edward Burston who had come round for one of his many chats about Fulham. When the time came for me to leave for the BBC studios, Edward said, "Come on, I'll get you out of this." We leapt outside into his Porsche. We sped off and all they got was a shot of his rear number plate. It read FU2. (Not necessarily a reference to Fulham.)

But Kathy and I weren't just a publicity story, the model and the DJ. We had a genuine love story. She was a smashing girl, and when we broke up there were no hard feelings. We kept in touch for a while, but after we parted she changed completely. The girl who would have legalised cannabis was now off drugs, off alcohol, no longer the party animal but spent time in meditation. I called her Kathy the chameleon.

After she left, I pondered if I really wanted to get married and have more children. Or was what I really wanted life on the road, where every day was an adventure and I never knew where I might end up?

The house Kathy found had two 13s in the postcode. The house number was 13 and the area code was SW13. Was it unlucky? I felt it might be when in the early days there, while I was away working in Ireland, there was an elaborate attempt at a break-in. Someone had cut the wires to the burglar alarm. As it went off, he submerged it in a dustbin that he had filled with water to mute the sound. By a 1000 to 1 chance a girl delivering the evening newspaper heard the muted sound, tipped the bin on its side and the alarm went off at full tilt. The burglar, by now in the back garden ready to break in, scarpered.

I'd not been at the new house long when someone sprayed a swastika on the side of my Rolls outside. Someone else, or maybe the same person, painted the word MOD in big letters on my front door. Was there some hidden message that I wasn't getting?

Driving home from Thames after midnight one night, I was followed by a police car all the way to the door of my house. "Excuse me, sir," said the police sergeant. "Have you been drinking?"

"Not at all, sergeant," I said. "I've been working very

hard. But if you'd care to have one, you're welcome to step inside."

Thus began a long friendship with Sergeant Len Rees, which survives to this day. Len was based at Barnes nick where there was a very nice snooker table that he invited me to play on. In return, he and some of his mates would come round and play on my pool table (not quite in the same league). I told him about the elaborate attempt at a break-in and that I was worried about the vulnerability of the house when I was away a lot, so he said he would keep an eye on it. It turned out that he was a Fulham supporter and, in exchange for a couple of matchday tickets, he would leave a police car outside my house when I was away at weekends. You couldn't get more security than that.

There wouldn't be a hope in hell of that kind of thing happening today. For a start, the police station in Barnes like so many others is long gone and Len is now on the South Coast, lamenting the fate of the police force he served so well, once having a knife stuck in his chest an inch from his heart when he went to arrest a man in a pub.

He and I often chuckle about another incident when I had a stalker. This woman looked me up in the phone directory, found an address in Barnes, turned up one day and threw a brick through the window. She got the wrong David Hamilton. This poor man was sitting there, minding his own business when this dirty great chunk of masonry, plus shattered glass, landed on his carpet. Sgt Rees was quickly on the scene. When the woman appeared in court in Kingston the next day, he gave his evidence in the deadpan way coppers do.

"When I asked her why she did it, she said, 'It's that David Hamilton'. 'Which David Hamilton?' I asked.

'You know, the one on the radio.' 'And why did you throw a brick through his window?' – To which she replied, 'It's none of your fucking business.'" (Cue stifled laughter in court.)

So the judge said, "You would not tell the officer, but you will tell me in my courtroom – why did you do it?"

The woman said, "It's none of your fucking business either."

A few weeks later the same woman turned up at Broadcasting House. Paul Burnett, who was unlucky enough to look a bit like me, was leaving the building when she ran up behind him and threw a can full of yellow paint over him. He was covered from head to toe in yellow paint and looked like a canary.

"Take that, David Hamilton!" she shouted.

Paul whirled round and said, "But I'm Paul Burnett."

Once again she hung around and was arrested. When she appeared in the local court, the judge mentioned her previous offence and said, "You've got the wrong man twice." When pressed for her reasons for doing it, she said, "It's the things he says on the radio."

"Like what?" asked the judge.

"Things like – smack botties."

Paul Burnett and I would laugh about it in the future, but what if it had been acid, rather than paint? Sometimes the connection between presenter and listener can get a little too close. My stalker was given a week in Holloway to dissuade her from any more attacks. And I deleted smack botties from my repertoire.

After my trip with them to America, Thames looked after me well. Two years running I hosted the *TV Times* Gala Awards. *TV Times* had a huge circulation in those days, before daily newspapers printed TV schedules, and their awards show was the big one of the year. In 1979

I hosted The World Disco Championships in Leicester Square for Thames. Because I was doing my radio show in the afternoon I couldn't do the dress rehearsal so the producer Steve Minchin offered to stand in for me. "I can trust you, can't I, to do the show without doing the dress run?" said Steve. I assured him he could.

Everything went swimmingly until the finale when I announced, "And now the World Disco Dancing Champion for 1969."

"Seventy-nine," chanted the crowd, and I hastily corrected it.

"You bloody fool," said Steve afterwards. "You've got 69 on the brain."

By 1980 there was exciting news. Thames were about to have a local news right after *News at Ten*. Naturally, having read news for Thames in America I expected to be asked to do it, at least on the two nights when I was on duty. But word came through that, although it would be done from the announcers' studio, it would be presented by an NUJ member and not an Equity one. This meant that while the announcers were doing their 30 or 45 seconds here and there through the evening, at 10 o'clock they would have to vacate the studio and go and sit in the dressing room while someone else did the meaty stuff. It also meant they wouldn't be seen at all between 9 o'clock and the close-down at around midnight. I decided that after 20 years of television announcing, starting at ABC in Didsbury, it was time to call it a day. So I left Thames for the second time, and this time there was no going back. A few years later they lost their licence to provide weekday programmes for London and announcers in vision became a thing of the past. After I had finished as a TV announcer and no longer had a vested interest, I was invited to speak at a conference in Birmingham about the value of announcers in vision – a friendly face, the feeling there was actually someone there when most of the programmes are recorded, station loyalty. Speaking against the motion was a woman from Southern Television who said viewers were distracted by their ties or their hair and didn't take notice of what they were saying. In that case, why have newsreaders in vision? Of course, it was all complete nonsense, disguising the fact that it was cheaper having announcers out of vision.

As I left Thames, ATV came up with a series for me to host called *Up for the Cup* that filled the ITV Saturday night light entertainment slot. In it two teams of variety acts competed against each other, representing the social clubs of football teams. The judging panel were well-known footballers and I was the referee, complete with whistle. It was a sort of talent show with a football flavour. It did very well for two of the entertainers who appeared on it – a young Bobby Davro, who launched a long-running career, and Jim Bowen, a schoolteacher turned comedian who was spotted on it and given the cult show *Bullseye*. Jim was a TV natural who just breezed his way through everything.

After *Up for the Cup* I was back on the road. With Kathy gone I was now a free agent. Often at gigs I'd meet women who would say, "Where are you staying tonight?" I would say either at a hotel or driving back to London. Some would say, "Oh, you don't want to do that. Why don't you stay at mine?" I got to know women in every part of the country. Sometimes they'd be in touch ahead of a gig. "I hear you're coming to town. Do you want to stay at my place?" A wonderful bonus – free accommodation.

Back in London I dated a couple of Penthouse Pets and an American air stewardess I met on a soccer tour to

Florida. I met the actress Trudi Van Dorn who invited me to see her in a West End show. Afterwards we went back to her place for what must have been the longest seduction ever. For hour after hour she played me her Dory Previn records, some of which I found rather depressing. Finally, at 6 a.m., we went to bed. Was it worth the wait? Of course.

I took another actress, Imogen Hassell, to an opening night, after which she suggested we drop in on Omar Sharif. Fresh from his success in *Doctor Zhivago*, he was staying at the Westbury Hotel. We went up to his suite where he was sitting up in bed dispensing champagne, surrounded by a number of acolytes.

"Am I a star?" he asked the gathering.

"Of course, you're a star," said somebody.

"You're a superstar," said someone else.

As the champagne flowed, his stardom increased. "You're a megastar," I said.

"David's right," said Omar. "I am a megastar. So why am I out of work?"

Still chuckling, Imo and I took a taxi back to her house in Fulham for what I hoped might be a fun night. As we walked in the front door, there standing at the top of the stairs was a man mountain that I recognised as Kenneth Ives, who played Hawkeye in the BBC version of *The Last of the Mohicans*. I could almost see the tomahawk in his hand. "Oh, it's you," he said. "That's alright."

I wasn't quite sure how to take that. But I didn't stay around for coffee.

By this time I had a new agent, Peter Prichard. His main acts were Jimmy Tarbuck and Bob Monkhouse. I was a huge fan of Bob. To me he was the ultimate game show host. But he was at his best when you saw him live on stage. Once I went to see him at Bailey's in Watford and had a drink with him and his wife Jackie before the show.

"A terrible thing happened last night," he told me in the dressing room. "I had a heckler in. You know me, I can handle hecklers."

"Nobody better," I said.

"I don't know what happened. Something inside me snapped. I walked over to his table and kicked him in the teeth. I was expecting him to come and find me after the show but his family must have whisked him away." It just goes to show that even the greatest have a breaking point.

Peter Prichard was friendly with Leslie Conn, the owner of the Bristol Suite in London, and he took me there one evening. There were lots of young women sitting at tables, many on their own. Over a glass of champagne, kindly supplied by Leslie, I asked him how it all worked. He explained that customers bought the girls a bottle of champagne (no doubt very costly) and the girls kept them company at the table. If the girls liked the men, they could make their own financial arrangements to take the situation further. The house made the money on the champagne. He invited one of the girls over to our table. She was stunning and for the purposes of this story we will call her Melanie. Over more on the house champagne I told her I found her very attractive but explained that I didn't pay for sex.

"No money need change hands," she said. "We could have an arrangement."

"What did you have in mind?" I asked.

"You open things, don't you, like supermarkets and shops?" I nodded. "Well, I'm launching a pet shop in Surrey. You could open that for me."

She asked me how much I charged. I told her and then asked what her going rate was.

She said, "I reckon that's five to one. So you give me one and I'll give you five."

"If it's OK, I'd like to collect the first one now," I said.

I have to confess that on the journey home I did wonder what I had let myself in for. I needn't have worried. We had a night of unbridled passion. In the morning she asked to see my diary so that she could fix a date for the shop opening a few weeks ahead.

Often she'd call me and say, "Hi, it's Mel. It's collection time." I think I had collected four by the time I turned up and opened her shop. That's it, I thought. But no, she rang again and said, "I still owe you one."

On the morning after number five, I said goodbye to her on the doorstep. "That's it, Mel," I said. "We're all square."

"You mean you don't want to see me anymore?."

"Well, we had our arrangement and a deal is a deal. This is what you do for work."

"And what do you do for work?"

"I play records."

"Do you play records when you're not working, just for fun."

"Of course."

"Well, that's what I do in my spare time. I do this for fun. Just call when you want to see me and I'll take an evening off."

I started seeing her regularly. One evening we watched the film *The Days of Wine and Roses* with tears rolling down our cheeks. I could feel myself falling in love with her. It was then that I thought – how would I feel if I was in love with her and she was sleeping with other men through the week? Before I got in too deep, time to end The Arrangement.

CHAPTER 17

Dreena and the Little Dog Angel

I hoped *Up for the Cup* would run for another season or maybe for a few years. Signs looked good early on, but it was not to be. Confusion with mixing football and showbusiness perhaps, or maybe the club acts weren't good enough. If it was me the bosses didn't like, they could have replaced me with someone else. Whatever the reason, it left me with no television contract for the first time in 20 years. So I had to content myself with guest appearances on shows like *Punchlines* with Lennie Bennett and *Celebrity Squares* with Bob Monkhouse.

Edward Burston died suddenly, and very young, leaving his girlfriend Emiko on her own in London. I invited her out for dinner. We talked about Edward and what a top bloke he was. We talked about the Machiavellian goings on at Fulham, and Emi talked about the period of mourning. I wasn't sure if it was the Jewish or Japanese period of mourning but I realised it was something to be respected.

About three months after Edward died she said to me, "Davey, do you find me attractive?"

"Yes, very," I said.

"Then why you no kiss me? Period of mourning over now," she said, pointedly.

So I kissed her. Thus began an affair during which I realised that Japanese women are skilled at keeping their men happy. Until one day she started talking about babies, as in her and me having them. "They'd be funny-looking things, Emi," I said.

"Oh no. English man and Japanese woman can have lovely babies."

I just couldn't imagine it, and once again I realised I didn't want any more children and it was not right to deny a woman her chance to have some. Time to say Sayonara.

So it was back on the road again. There were loads of clubs to play, but Radio 2 didn't play much disco music and I was relying on people remembering me from Radio 1 and *Top of the Pops*. The gigs were late, audiences were often drunk. But it was all I knew to make a living, and I still had a lot of bills to pay.

I had known Dee Shenderey since she was the first woman DJ on Radio Luxembourg. In time she became a successful songwriter, penning songs for Petula Clark and Charles Aznavour. She married Ken Shipman, owner of Twickenham Film Studios, and they had a succession

A star all her lifetime, Petula Clark

of beautiful country homes, to which I was often invited for weekends with whoever I was with at the time. Each home had a snooker table and a swimming pool. Every weekend spent there was magical. Dee was very witty, a great hostess. She and Ken had a cook/housekeeper and a chauffeur who would pick us up from the nearest station if we didn't want to drive. They had lovely dogs and a parrot called Enky who would greet people as they walked into the room with "Allo." I walked into the room and Enky said, "Fuck off." Everybody collapsed with laughter.

By the mid-'80s Dee and Ken were living in a beautiful house near the village of Cricket Malherbie in the shadow of Somerset's Quantock Hills. They were going to apply for a licence to run a local radio station. Dee, who could be very persuasive, knew that I had become disenchanted with the musical direction Radio 2 had taken and had the idea that she would be the managing director of the station which would be based in Taunton, and I would be the programme controller. What was I doing, even considering doing it? Thank goodness they didn't get the licence. I didn't know it then, of course, but stations like that would be gobbled up by big media groups in no time and the founders who had done all the hard work would get paid off with a few grand. Never do business with friends is a good lesson, I suppose. As Ken Shipman used to say, "A fool and his money are soon parted." Ken, a deep thinker, had another expression, "A human life is just a blink in the eye of a Time Lord." Ken and Dee, sadly, have had their blink but they knew how to live and I thank them for their wonderful hospitality and memorable times when they shared with me their fabulous lifestyle. And I thank my lucky stars that I didn't go into local radio with them.

In 1981, I found a lovely house of my own. Like the previous one, it was in Barnes but this time detached with a drive at the front for off street parking and a nice garden at the back. It wasn't in Ken and Dee's league but a nice London house, a short drive from Fulham's ground and half an hour from Broadcasting House. With five bedrooms it had plenty of space for guests and one room downstairs I turned into an office where Judy, my PA, handled all my mail, and travel arrangements. Less than ten years after saying goodbye to my house in Oxshott, I was back on my feet again.

Two years later some friends, Ray and Gwen Jenkins, fixed me up with a blind date. I always say that she needed to be blindfolded. All I knew about Dreena Shrager was that she was an aerobics teacher. I thought to myself, aerobics teachers are all flash and spend all their time going, "Woo…" All she knew about me was that I was a disc jockey and she felt they were flash, too. So neither of us had any great expectations on the day.

I first saw her outside the Paris Theatre in Lower Regent Street where I had been doing a show. When she got out of the car she looked pretty tall, so I said to myself, "That's the end of that. She won't be interested in me." We went on to an Italian restaurant in St Martin's Lane where waiters danced with the women customers. She was obviously a good dancer and liked having a good time. It turned out she was doing 17 one-hour dance classes a week. She was certainly in great shape.

When we went back to my house later for a drink, she asked me what I was doing at the moment. I told her I had just done a recording for big screen videos. These were reckoned to be the next big thing in discos: you'd dance to the record while seeing the band on the big screen. When I asked if she'd like to see it she said, "Yes."

The recording had been organised by my old pal Tony Williams from the Showbiz XI and was done in a studio in Essex. "You record the links to camera," said Tony. "And we'll drop the clips in later." He showed me the script:

"Hi. I'm David Hamilton. And everything looks better on the big screen. For example this…"

(Clip of horse racing.)

"Or this…"

(Shots of big crowds at football.)

"Or even this…"

(Shots of a pop group on stage.)

There was more, but not much. In other words, a doddle.

I hadn't seen it yet so I put it in the video player and we sat back to watch it.

"Everything looks better on the big screen" I said. "For example, this…"

(Cut to a shot of a woman with the biggest boobs you've ever seen.)

"Or this…"

(Shot of a man with an enormous penis.)

Or even this…"

(Shot panning down the body of a hermaphrodite.)

Before I could remove the video, she said, "I think I'll have my coat now," and walked out of the door.

The following morning I rang Ray Jenkins. "What did she say about me?"

"She thought you were nice but is shocked that you're making porn videos."

I rang her and said it was a spoof video to make me laugh and that Tony Williams assured me this was the only rude copy. She took some convincing. It turned out that she was separated from her husband and had three children and she told me that most of the men she had met since leaving her husband had turned out to be weirdos, and she felt that here was another one.

I met her children Angela, Simon and Charlotte for the first time that Christmas. They'd been shopping in the West End and came along to see me at my pitch on Oxford Street where I was doing a 48-hour 'Chatathon' on Christmas Eve and Christmas Day with Judy Kaye to raise money for the children's charity Judy worked for. The children all seemed nice and well behaved. As it was the season of goodwill, people gave generously to the cause. Actually, we were all quite brave to do it because an IRA bomb had gone off outside Harrods just a week before, killing several people. We didn't quite make the 48 hours because around 8 o'clock on Christmas night the goodwill ran out: there was a bomb warning, and police cleared the area. Probably just as well, as I was standing in for Terry Wogan on the breakfast show on Boxing Day morning. Talk about jet lag.

After the supposed porn video there was another incident that could have been taken as an omen that could finish our budding relationship. On a freezing February evening Dreena drove round to my house, as I had planned to take her out for dinner. I was sitting in my office at the front of the house, waiting for her to arrive, when I heard a crash. My first thought was that it could be her. Thought two: it's a busy road with lots of traffic, why would it be her? Thought three: if she was turning into the house, it could well be her.

When I stepped outside I realised indeed it was. She had been turning right into the house and a cab driver coming the other way hit her head-on, so that her car was facing the direction it had come from. I could see from the skid marks that he was well over the speed limit. We pushed her car into the driveway. Good thing it was a Volvo or it could have been written off. She waved away the ambulance that turned up, saying she was fine, but I could see she was shaken. I got her into the house to get warm and asked if she would like a tea or a glass of wine. She opted for the wine and I opened a bottle of red. I was in shock, too, and we drank the wine on an empty stomach.

"We'll have to forget the dinner," she said. "You'd better get me home."

We set off in my car to her home in Tadworth. On the A3 I could see some flashing blue lights behind me and a police car indicated to me to pull into a lay by. "Excuse me, sir," said the policeman. "I've stopped you because you were weaving in the road. Have you been drinking?"

"This lady has been involved in a road accident," I explained. "We had a drink to settle our nerves and now I'm driving her home."

"I'll have to ask you to blow in this bag," he said. It seemed an eternity before I got the result. I was standing there freezing and shaking and thinking this evening has been a disaster. Eventually he said, "You are what is called a borderline case." I avoided coming up with a witty retort. "Obviously, you've been drinking, sir, so I recommend you leave the car here and take a taxi for the rest of your journey."

How our relationship survived that night I will never know.

Survive it we did and, apart from anything else, we did a lot of talking – something we were both very good at.

One day when she left the house, I looked out of the French windows into the garden and it was pouring with rain. It summed up my feelings. I realised that I missed her and decided there and then that I would ask her to move in with me. When I did, she warned me of the reality of living with three of somebody else's children. She was right, of course. Delightful though they could be, there were always fights. It wasn't easy for them, living with a man who wasn't their father. Any two of them could fight at any time. At times it was World War 3. Gwen Jenkins told me that if Dreena moved in, life would never be dull. And she was right.

There was one incident that is very distressing to relive. The *News of the World*, of all newspapers, wanted to do a photo shoot at the house of 'DH, the family man'. Lots of jolly photos were taken in the house and garden of the five of us. At some point, someone (apparently it was me, though I don't remember doing it) opened the front door and the family's Jack Russell ran out into the busy main road. Moments later an Indian man came to the door with the dead dog in his arms. "I'm so sorry. I've run over your dog."

When the jolly photos appeared in the *News of the World* a few days later they were not the cause of celebration that was hoped for. The family that had just moved in nearly moved out again.

Bringing up three children who are not your own is not easy for you, or them. Then there was another addition to the Hamilton household. After the tragic incident with their Jack Russell, there was lots of pressure to have another dog. "A dog wouldn't fit in with our lifestyle, with us always being away," I said.

I was lying in the bath one day when into the room came Dreena holding this little furry red puppy. The puppy looked at me and sniffed as if to say, "Who are you?" And I looked at her as if to say, "And who are you?"

"This is Rosie Hamilton," said Dreena. Rosie, it turned out, was a Labrador/Red Setter cross who was one of a litter at Simon's school. I discovered later that she had been hidden in the utility room for several days. So much for my word meaning anything in the house. I had to play the tough guy so for at least two days I said, "She can't stay here. She'll have to go back." Secretly, I knew she had melted my heart and that if she was going to stay with us I would make sure she would have a wonderful life.

Rosie turned out to be the perfect dog. She didn't bark for no reason. In fact, she hardly barked at all, so life with her was peaceful. She was so intelligent that I think she worked out how I wanted her to be, and she became that dog. She travelled on trains and boats and planes and loved all of them. We went by train to Plymouth to appear on a TV show called *That's My Dog*. The premise of the show was that members of the public had to guess who the famous owner of the dog was. Before the show, we gave her some exercise with a walk along Plymouth Hoe. She was a stunning dog and people stopped to admire her. Then, when it came to the show, the contestants said to the host Derek Hobson, "Oh, we know whose dog that is. We've just seen her on Plymouth Hoe," which sort of defeated the object of the programme.

When we went to Alderney for a weekend, Aurigny Airlines gave her a seat for the price of a child's ticket. Flying back to Southampton on the Sunday night, she had the window seat and I had the aisle seat. She looked out of the window at the sea and as we approached land she turned to me. "It's the land, Rosie," I said. As we lost height, my ears popped. I thought hers might be doing the same so I stroked her back. She looked at me affectionately. As we landed, she looked at me again, as though to say, "We've landed safely." By now people on the plane were looking at us and smiling, as though we were a couple.

She loved going on motorboats, open-top buses, the Bluebell Railway where the ticket inspector gave her her own ticket; she joined us on a half-marathon walk for charity around the streets of London and headed another charity walk, 'Promenading the Dog', in Worthing where she made sure she stayed in front of all the other dogs and owners. She sat in the audience when I compered the Rescue Dog of the Year show and other canine events, though she was dying to get up on stage with me. At one of these shows someone noticed her lovely calm personality and we were asked if she could be a 'Pat Dog'. This involved her going to hospitals where patients who were missing their own dogs were allowed to stroke her, which invariably made them feel better and helped to cheer them up. Always she behaved impeccably.

Rosie turned out to be the catalyst for so many things. One of the people we met at doggy events was Katie Boyle. Many years earlier, when I was a teenager, Katie had been the first TV star I had ever seen. She was waiting for a taxi on Putney Bridge and I was blown away by how beautiful she was. I couldn't tell her she was my secret teenage crush when she asked me if I'd like to join her on the management committee of Battersea Dogs Home. It was an unpaid job but something I thought was really worthwhile. We went regularly to meetings at Battersea and often as well to the country kennels at Ascot. Katie once left a message on my answerphone that caused a certain amount of merriment: "David, I'll drive if you'll hold my Chihuahuas." I spent ten years on the management committee at Battersea until a radio contract took me out of town during the week and made it impossible for me to get to meetings.

Rosie on the Bluebell Railway

Because of Rosie we went to lots of doggie events and for some years I wrote a column in *Dogs Monthly* magazine about R and R – rescue and rehoming. We walked everywhere – she was tireless, and she loved to swim in the sea. We walked a lot in Richmond Park where we often bumped into fellow dog walkers, Bruce Welch from The Shadows and Greg Lake from Emerson, Lake and Palmer.

Often I would take a tennis ball and a racquet with me. I'd knock the ball as high into the sky as I could. She'd stand under it and catch it in her mouth. She caught it every time. She had lots of endearing habits. When I came home she'd grab my wrist and take me where she wanted me in the house. She never bit me or hurt me. I knew I could trust her completely. Sometimes I was dying to go to the loo but I knew it meant a lot to her, her way of claiming me.

Rosie lived to nearly sixteen, a good age for a big dog. When she died I cried for an entire weekend. She was an angel and she bonded a family together. After she died I took my usual walk in Richmond Park. It just wasn't the same without her. It was a fine day but as I looked up I saw a rainbow. One end of the rainbow seemed to be where our house was, about two miles away. Sometime later I found this poem by Norah M Holland, 'The Little Dog Angel'.

High up in the courts of Heaven today a little dog angel awaits.
With the other angels he will not play, but he sits alone at the gates.
"For I know that my master will come", says he.
"And when he comes he will call for me".
He sees the spirits that pass him by as they hasten towards the throne
And he watches them with a wistful eye as he sits at the gates alone.
"But I know that if I just wait patiently that some day my master will come", says he.
And his master, far on the earth below, as he sits in his easy chair
Forgets sometimes, and he whistles low for the dog that is not there
And the little dog angel cocks his ears, and dreams that his master's call he hears
And I know when at length his master waits outside in the dark and cold

For the hand of Death to open the gates that lead to their courts of gold
The little dog angel's eager bark will comfort his soul in the shivering dark.

CHAPTER 18

To Friends

DAVE Eastwood, who had been with me at the Compton Forces Network in RAF Compton Bassett while doing our National Service in 1958, was a late starter in radio. For a while he was a lay preacher but by his late twenties he was doing some DJ-ing in discos and then landed a job at his local station, Radio City in Liverpool. From there he progressed to Radio Luxembourg. When he started working for Luxembourg in London he rented a place in Putney, not far from me, close enough for us to meet up again. I saw quite a bit of Dave. He was a lively character and good company, but I got a shock when he left a message on my answerphone. I had to play it back twice to make sure I had heard it right. Sadly, I had. He was in the leukaemia ward of the London Hospital. As soon as we could, Dreena and I set off to the old hospital in the Whitechapel Road that dated back to the Industrial Revolution. We found Dave in a public ward surrounded by men, most of whom were coughing and looked as though they were dying of cancer. Some of them were quite young. It was a most depressing sight. As we left, it was pouring with rain. I took a packet of cigarettes from my pocket and threw it in the gutter. I vowed there and then that I would never smoke again. It was difficult because I was hooked on cigarettes. I conquered the nicotine craving by sucking Polo mints.

Dave left hospital and a few months later we went to his 50th birthday party in Southend, where he'd been working for BBC Radio Essex. At his party he made a speech where he said, "One of the good things about my illness is that my oldest friend has given up smoking." More inspiration for me to keep off the fags. I couldn't let him down.

Dave fought the good fight. He went through a lot, having his blood and his bone marrow changed. Sadly, he lost his fight and passed away at the age of 50. He was six weeks younger than me. The shock of his illness and the people I saw in the London Hospital made me give up smoking. How crazy was I to smoke when both of my parents died of lung cancer in their fifties? And yet nothing he had done brought about the illness that killed him. Life can be very cruel. Those who heard him knew he was a terrific broadcaster. He achieved that ambition we had during our National Service days and spent his short life doing the job he loved. Without him, I almost certainly wouldn't be here today. God bless you, Dave, and thank you for giving me the gift of a long life.

I've been lucky to have good friends. Another mate was Robin McGibbon, who I first met when his company, Everest Books, published two books of mine back in the '70s – *David Hamilton's Beauty Tips for Women* and *Make Ends Meet*, economy tips during tough financial times based on features on my radio shows. Robin shared my love of football and played semi-professionally for Redhill. He was a Charlton supporter and, like me, had marvelled at the antics of the great Sam Bartram when he was a boy. He invited me along to the unveiling of Sam's nine-foot statue at The Valley. It was wonderful to see my boyhood hero being honoured in this way. Some time later, Robin arranged for me to go to The

Valley to present a pair of boys' football boots to go to an impoverished children's charity in South Africa on the TV programme *London Tonight*. As I gave the boots to Lee Simons, wife of the chairman of Charlton Athletic, there was a surprise visitor. Robin had contacted Sam Bartram's daughter Moira and persuaded her to fly from her home in Canada to give me the three scrapbooks I had kept of Sam when I was a boy and which I gave him at a charity match he had organised and which I played in at Derby County. Sam, I discovered, had treasured the books and kept them under glass on his sitting room table. When he died, Moira took them with her to Canada. She handed them to me in front of the *London Tonight* cameras with one proviso: eventually they would go to the Charlton Museum. What a lovely thing for Robin and Moira to do.

When I re-read the scrapbooks they took me right back to those boyhood days of seeing the most exciting footballer I ever watched. I kept them at home for a long time and when I felt the time was right I handed them over to the Charlton Museum. I was thrilled to know they thought they were worth keeping. They were, I suppose, a chronicle of the man who played more times for Charlton than anyone else, their finest player. One day, hopefully, the club in London SE7 will return to the top division where it was in Sam Bartram's glory days.

Robin McGibbon became a very successful author. One of his books was about the notorious Kray twins. When I was doing a gig on the Isle of Wight, Reggie Kray asked Robin if I would visit him in Parkhurst Prison. I gave it some thought and then decided against it. Why would I condone a hardened criminal?

Some time later, in all innocence, I read out a request on Radio 2 from a Reggie in Maidstone. Subsequently

I discovered that Reg Kray had been moved from Parkhurst to Maidstone prison. I should have rumbled it when the song he asked for was 'Jailhouse Rock'.

I made lots of friends among the Fulham players. Bobby Moore asked me to do the opening night disco of his club, Mooro's, in Stratford. Alan Mullery, Les Strong and Freddie Callaghan came to my 70th birthday party. Freddie and his wife Hazel holidayed with us in Mallorca. Back in his playing days he was known as The Tank. He played the game hard but fairly. The only time he was sent off was for fighting Terry Venables. After a spell of managing Brentford and Woking, he became a taxi driver, a fate that befell a lot of players at that time. If he saw me in London, he'd give me a lift and refuse to take any money. If we were both going to a Fulham event, he'd run me there. He was that kind of guy. When you look at footballers today stepping off coaches wearing headphones and on their mobile phones, you realise that Freddie was the last of a dying breed – and one of the most genuine people I ever met.

I think football changed dramatically with the start of the new millennium. Until then, supporters were often earning more than the players. I was one of the committee that organised the testimonial of Fulham captain Simon Morgan. We raised over £100,000 for him, which he was delighted to have. Gradually, in the 2000s foreign owners were coming in, foreign players were coming in and the game was awash with money. Some players were earning Simon's testimonial money in a week. In the Premier League I can't see there will be any more testimonials.

I played football until I was fifty. My last game was at Maidstone where I was carried off the pitch after being kicked on the knee. In the dressing room Barry Fry, the

Maidstone manager, put an ice pack on my knee. After a painful minute or two, he said, "Now see if you can bend it."

I realised that if I couldn't I was in trouble and thought about the work I had lined up in the coming weeks.

When I found I could bend it, he said, "Now get out there and run it off."

Driving me home, Dreena said, "Time to call it a day, I think. Injuries from now will be harder to shake off."

So I decided on a non-contact game. Despite suggestions from pals like Pete Murray and Jess Conrad to take up golf, I opted for tennis, which took less time. After playing with friends and family, I graduated to charity matches at venues like the Vanderbilt Club, Queen's Club and Beckenham. I foolishly challenged Piers Morgan to a match, ignoring the fact that he was over 20 years younger and six inches taller than me. The next day pictures appeared in his column of him looking triumphant and me looking knackered. He beat me 6-2, 6-1. To be honest, In the second set I was lucky to get 1.

CHAPTER 19

Macca and Cilla

PAUL McCartney wrote the song 'The Long and Winding Road'. He wasn't happy with the finished product because John Lennon brought in Phil Spector who added strings and a choir, which Paul didn't like. I thought it was one of the most beautiful records I'd ever heard.

I first met Paul when I interviewed the Beatles on *ABC at Large* in 1963. In the '70s I was enjoying a brilliant concert by Junior Walker and the All Stars at the Rainbow Theatre, Finsbury Park. During the interval someone in the row behind tapped me on the shoulder and said, "It's Diddy David." I turned round and saw it was Paul McCartney. My female companion was enormously impressed.

When I moved house some years later I was going through some cartridges that contained some old jingles. On one was a short voice track that said simply, "Hi, this is Paul McCartney. Where's David Hamilton?" Clearly it had been recorded in a BBC studio and it didn't need a genius to work out that Paul was there, and I wasn't. I wracked my brain to try to remember what had happened and how I missed him. Had I been late arriving back from a gig the night before? Did he not hang around long after the agreed time of recording? Whatever the answers, the outcome was that I stood up arguably the greatest pop star of all. After all this time, I can only apologise to Sir Paul.

I have to say missing me didn't do his career much harm.

Somehow I survived Paul's friend Cilla Black. Let me put that another way. I survived being on her TV show.

When I was booked to appear on the *Cilla Black Show*, the producer came up with the bright idea that I would go into a cage with a lion and tell it a joke to make it roar with laughter. What joke should I tell the lion? Something it might relate to.

When I was let into the cage there was the lion sitting on a huge plinth. I stood there – some distance away, I should add – and told the lion this joke:

A man wants to be a lion trainer so he goes to the expert to seek advice.

"You're in the ring with a whip in your hand," says the lion trainer. "You go towards the lion, crack the whip and say, 'Sit'."

"Supposing he doesn't sit?" says the trainee.

"In that case, pick up the chair, walking towards him with the chair, legs towards him, and say firmly, 'Sit'."

"Supposing he still doesn't sit?"

"In that case, pick up some manure in the ring and throw it in his eyes."

"Supposing there's no manure in the ring?" says the man.

"There will be," says the lion trainer.

The lion yawned.

They dubbed in the roar later.

Which reminds me of another circus story.

Dreena and I were in Malta where I was judging the Maltese entries for the Eurovision Song Contest. An Italian circus was on the island and some friends

196

suggested we pay it a visit. I was interested in the circus world since my days of hosting it for ITV. I regarded it as another branch of show business. What I didn't know was that Mrs H didn't share my enthusiasm, as she thought much of it was cruel to animals. I was hell-bent on going and, as anybody who knows me will say, when I set my heart on doing something, nothing will change my mind.

During the interval, we were invited to join the owners for a drink. Unknown to me, Dreena asked them if they had a knife throwing act, because it was something I particularly enjoyed. At the end of the interval, they suggested we might like to join them in the VIP area on the edge of the ring. How nice, I thought. As the second half began, sure enough there was the knife thrower, along with his bikini clad assistant. It was a pretty impressive act. As the knives went in, one after the other, the assistant didn't move a muscle.

Suddenly, the knife thrower called for a volunteer from the audience. A huge spotlight shone on the VIP box.

"Englishman…" shouted the knife thrower.

I looked round at the audience behind me.

"He means you," said Dreena, pushing me forward.

"No, there are lots of English people here," I said. "He could mean anyone."

The next thing I knew, the assistant was grabbing my hand and leading me into the sawdust ring. A big hood was put over my head and my arms and legs were mana-cled to the circular board, which the assistant spun a few times until I was completely dizzy. Some balloons were placed at strategic places near my feet and hands, with another one between my legs.

A roll on the drums and I felt one of the knives slam

into the balloon by my right hand. Thump. Bang. Next it was the left hand. Then the right foot and the left foot. All that remained was the one between my legs. Oh no, not the wedding tackle, I thought. Another thump and a bang and then the assistant spun the wheel again before removing the hood from my head.

As I walked back to the box though the sawdust, my legs had turned to jelly, my suntan disappeared and my face was ashen. I survived the night of the long knives.

After that, we never went to the circus again.

CHAPTER 20

To Anguilla

T RUST me when I say this. There are people who appear on television who are accepted by the world as charming and lovely who are really as hard as nails and actually rather nasty. They are good actors. And then there was Jeremy Beadle. Not everybody liked Jeremy, possibly because he played tricks on people and appeared to take the mickey out of them. I got to know Beadle after appearing on his show *Game for a Laugh*. I took the opportunity to invite him to play for the Showbiz XI. Say the word charity and Beadle was your man. I'm not sure if he had played football before, but

In the Showbiz XI dressing room with Jeremy Beadle

once he knew our matches were for charity, he became a regular member of the team. We became good friends with Jeremy and his wife Sue and holidayed together in Mallorca. He was great company and he knew everybody. When he threw a party, the house was packed. He knew the value of networking. At one party we went to there was Alan Sugar, Gerald Ronson, David Dein – from the club Beadle supported, Arsenal – Richard Littlejohn, Greg Dyke, Chris Tarrant... The room was full of faces.

In 1985 he produced a TV pop quiz series called *Pop the Question*, recorded at TVS in Southampton and aired on Channel 4. He chose Lee Peck as the host and Chris Tarrant and me as team captains, with two pop star guests on each panel. The shows were a hoot to do and, as is often the case, led on to something else with the same company. Before that came other exciting news. W H Smith had branched out into the new satellite television business and were launching two new channels, Screensport and Lifestyle, a channel aimed at women at home during the day. George Black Junior remembered me from Tyne-Tees TV during his father's time running it and chose me as the main presenter for Lifestyle. This involved one long day in the Molinare studio in Soho to record a week of programmes. Once again there were continuity links to record in vision, then all sorts of programmes involving cookery, fashion, new video releases and other items of interest to women. There was a daily 'Coffee Break' at 11 o'clock where I interviewed celebrity guests. I had a different coloured sweater for each day and would change between each 10-minute show. Including changing time, we recorded the five shows in just over an hour. Most of the shows went smoothly until I interviewed the actress Jane Asher. On the Monday show when I mentioned her relationship with Paul McCartney she stormed out of the studio. Back in her dressing room the producers tried to placate her and convince her to stay. Apparently, she had told a researcher that the subject of Macca was taboo. If anybody had told me that, I would certainly have steered clear of it – but nobody did. If she'd said in the studio, "Sorry, we agreed not to go there," I'd have stopped right there and we'd have edited it out. Instead we lost minutes of studio time while she was being cajoled into staying around and carrying on. When she came back for the Tuesday and Wednesday shows there was a decided frost. It was only towards the end of the week that she warmed up a little while talking about cakes and quilt-making.

The guest I was most excited to meet was Roy Orbison, I suppose because he seemed to have been there throughout my life and one of the first records I bought was 'Only the Lonely'. As he sat opposite me wearing those famous shades, I marvelled quietly at the fact that I could be in the same studio as the legendary Big O. What a nice man, what a voice and what a talent. It was one of his last interviews and when he died not long after, a clip of it was shown on the ITN News.

Sue Kerr, former LWT announcer Sue Peacock, was the executive producer at Lifestyle TV and had an uncanny knack of finding new talent. She gave Dale Winton his TV break, which without doubt led him to doing *Supermarket Sweep*. She brought in Baz Bamigboye from the *Daily Mail* to do theatre and Andrew Morton to do royal gossip some time before he did his bestselling book on Princess Diana. After the long recording day Sue, her husband Andrew and I would have dinner at Phood, the restaurant next to the studios. Sometimes Andrew Morton would join us and tell us the real gossip, the stuff that was too hot to do on the TV show. One evening he said, "Diana is convinced that she could be involved in an accident, that a boat might blow up or a plane could fall out of the sky." He told us about Barry Mannakee, the police officer with the Royal Protection Squad who was her bodyguard and who she became very close to. He was killed in a motorcycle accident in 1987 and Diana believed he was bumped off. When Dreena and I heard the news of Diana's death in that dreadful car accident in Paris on that Sunday morning in 1997, I remembered what Andrew had told me.

After the 10-minute 'Coffee Breaks' at Lifestyle, something meatier came along. Sue Kerr came up with the idea of a 30 -minute programme in which I would tackle controversial issues like fox hunting and the value of the Royal Family. It was called *David Hamilton's People* and for the first time I had my name in a TV programme title.

Meanwhile, over at Radio 2, a new controller had taken over who seemed determined to take the station in a backward direction. Frances Line was married to the station's folk music presenter, Jim Lloyd, who years before I had taken over from as an announcer at Tyne-Tees. She brought out a document outlining Radio 2's future music policy that sounds hilarious today and was no less so then. She wanted a nostalgia package that included pan pipes, whistling and Wurlitzers, while there was no mention of Motown, surely the biggest nostalgia package of all, with its enormous catalogue of artists. So many listeners wrote to me – it was all letters in those days – saying they didn't like my music any more. I was so angry to see the station moving in such a wrong direction that I jumped ship and joined a commercial station based in Reading to do a daily show for them, plus a weekly show that they networked to a dozen other stations. Many people couldn't understand why I jumped out of a national show into a local one, but the reason was that it gave me the chance to play the music I knew most listeners wanted.

From day one, with the extra problems of commercials on cartridges cluttering up the studio, of split breaks where some commercials went out on one transmitter and others on another, I wondered what I had done. I also lost out on so much other work. I had just done the Eurovision Song Contest Preview Show (British entries) for BBC TV. They didn't ask me again after I left Radio 2.

I had devised a programme for the light entertainment division of Radio 2. The producer came up with the title, 'Some of These Days'. The premise of the show is that it featured events that had happened on the date that it was to be transmitted. With me as the host a panel of four celebrities would answer questions about that day, illustrated with music, newsreel soundtrack, etc. It occurred to me when I came up with the idea that, if successful on radio, it would transfer well on to television. We recorded the shows at the Paris Theatre in Lower Regent Street during my final year at Radio 2. Because the producer had a certain amount of input, I waived a creator fee and settled for payment as the show host. After I left Radio 2, the producer phoned me and said they were doing another series of *Some of These Days* but, in view of my departure, they wouldn't be able to use me as the host any more. It came as quite a surprise to see, not too long after this, a television show hosted by Martyn Lewis called *Today's The Day*. It ran for some time on daily BBC television and was a TV adaptation of my radio format. Ironically, I was booked as a guest panellist on one of the shows.

"What a great idea this is," I said to the producer.

"Whose idea was it?" No one seemed to know. Funny, that.

After leaving both Thames and Radio 2, I was back on my feet again in the early '90s. After two years at Radio 210 in Reading, the opportunity came to join the newly launched Capital Gold, a golden oldies station in London that also boasted the likes of Tony Blackburn, Kenny Everett and Mike Read. So I was doing a daily morning show there, plus my daily recorded stints on Lifestyle TV, and then came along the chance to host an ITV game show. I was shown a video of an American show called *Million Dollar Chance of a Lifetime*. In the edition I saw, a couple actually won a million dollars. A net over their heads opened and they were showered with (in fact, counterfeit) money. It was very spectacular. TVS had bought the rights to the show here and three pilot shows were recorded at their studios in Southampton, one with Simon Bates, one with Nick Owen and the third with me. So I had a one-in-three chance of getting it. We opened the champagne at home when we found out after some wait that I was the chosen one.

When it came to recording the shows in Southampton, I learned that the Television Authority decreed that we couldn't give away a million pounds because we couldn't have a show that appealed to peoples' avarice. Instead of *Chance of a Lifetime*, the show would be called *All Clued Up*, and the maximum winnings would be £5000. So not quite the sensation I might have hoped for. *All Clued Up*, which featured two married couples playing against each other, was transmitted on the ITV network on Sunday afternoons, mainly in the summer. Because TVS was one of the smaller stations, it lacked the clout of the big ones, Thames, LWT and Granada, and the show went out in different time slots, often because of sport, and never a regular one. Despite this, we ran for three years on Sunday afternoons and then for one year on a Monday to Friday afternoon slot. We did 100 shows in all. A couple of years after *All Clued Up*, ITV launched a show called *Who Wants to Be a Millionaire*, where from time to time they gave away a million pounds. Worries about avarice had apparently flown out of the window.

On the set of All Clued Up

Dreena and I, plus her kids, had been living together for ten years, during which time she was still married to her first husband. (I was not the cause of the break up. They were living apart when we met.) Finally, her divorce came through and we decided we would get married. But where? Since it was the second time for both of us, a church wedding was out of the question. The obvious choice was Chelsea Town Hall. The previous year I had been the best man at the wedding of my friend and fellow Fulham supporter Alex Shooter and his wife Kim when they got married on Sandy Island, a tropical island off the coast of Anguilla in the Caribbean. It was such a brilliant venue that I thought I would copy their choice and do the same. The Anguillan link came from Les Strong, the ex-Fulham captain who was living out there and coaching the Anguillan football team. Les booked us into a great hotel. On the big day we took a boat out to the island which had several palm trees and a bar. That evening we had dinner for two on a jetty overlooking the ocean.

We flew back via Antigua. At the airport bar we bumped into Eric Clapton.

"This is my new bride", I said to Eric.

"David always plays 'Wonderful Tonight' for me on the radio," said Dreena.

Dreena and David with Sir Tim Rice,
Elaine Paige and Pete Murray

Eric said, "I wrote that for my wife Pattie Boyd. I hope it brings you better luck than it brought me."

When we got back to England we thought we ought to throw a party for all our friends who couldn't be at the wedding. We went to the opening night of the American entertainer Buddy Greco's three-week season at the Café Royal in Regent Street. After the show we met Buddy, who I had long been an enormous fan of, and also the manager of the Café Royal, Patrick. What, I asked Patrick, were the chances of us booking the room for a night while Buddy was here? He said he could juggle some dates to make it happen. The next day we rang round some pals and working colleagues. Nearly everyone said, "Yes," and on the night everyone had drinks and dinner and Buddy entertained us royally. What a great singer and pianist he was, supported by his wife Lesley Anders with her tribute to Peggy Lee. Buddy, who by now was in his eighties, finished his act with a superb version of 'MacArthur Park', which Jimmy Webb had written on Buddy's piano. Buddy Greco always loved England and spent the last years of his working life living in Westcliff-on-Sea. Aged nearly 90, he did a double on New Year's Eve, playing Ronnie Scott's and The Savoy. A remarkable man and a great cabaret entertainer.

Having established a nice relationship with the Café Royal, we were back there a few years later when Jeremy Beadle organised a '40 Years in Showbiz' night for me, sponsored by *OK* magazine, where pals like P J Proby and Craig Douglas sang for me. What a night. I would never have guessed then that I would go on to do 60-plus.

CHAPTER 21

Showtime at Fulham

E VERYTHING came to an end at the same time. TVS lost their contract, so that was the end of *All Clued Up*. W H Smith decided they didn't want to be in television anymore and pulled the plug on Lifestyle and Screensport – a shame, because they were just beginning to take off. W H Smith were pioneers of satellite television. This was before you started to see dishes on houses all over the country. They were ahead of their time. A couple more years, and they would have seen significant audiences.

By mutual consent, Capital Gold and I parted company in 1994. It was not a happy partnership. Capital Radio had a programme controller who presided over two stations, Capital FM and Capital Gold. Though Gold boasted the star names, his priorities and those of the sales people were very much with the FM station, which was aimed at younger listeners. Gold, on 1548 AM, had a weaker signal which disappeared when cars were in tunnels. Audiences generally were gravitating to the newer and better FM, and listening figures for AM radio were diminishing everywhere. It was an uphill battle, not made easier by the fact that the controller was unduly sensitive about Gold playing records that were on the FM playlist.

To try to keep the PC happy, I'd agreed a year before to do a Sunday lunchtime show for XTRA AM, another station in the Capital stable and based in Birmingham. Thus every Sunday morning I'd hammer up the M40 motorway to the Midlands to broadcast from the studios in Aston that I remembered from my days at ABC TV. Most of my meagre fee went on the petrol money. I did that for another month after I finished with Capital in London. When I walked out of Capital Tower in the Euston Road for the last time, I didn't have a job in radio to look forward to but once word got out that I had left, two offers came in from former BBC radio producers I had worked happily with in the past, Geoff Mullin and Chris Vezey. Geoff by now was head of music at Melody Radio, a beautiful music station owned by Lord Hanson which pretty much played his favourite records. Chris was running Classic FM. Both were offering me daily shows. Dreena was keen that I should join Classic as she loved classical music. I wasn't so sure. I enjoying hearing it from time to time but knew very little about it. One thing I did know was that there were lots of foreign composers and I might struggle pronouncing their names. Chris reassured me that Classic had a pronunciation unit who would put me right. "Henry Kelly," he told me, "started out talking about Beath-oven." Maybe that was the Irish pronunciation.

On the other hand, I'd had thirty years' experience of talking about pop music and had built up a good knowledge of it. My inclination was to plump for Melody. The one drawback I could see was that up to that point Melody presenters had been allowed zero personality. A case of "That was... and this is...". Their adverts on the side of London buses had said, MELODY – RADIO WITHOUT THE SPEAKERS, as though disc jockeys were the kiss of death. All that was about to change, Geoff assured me, and so was the music, which had been largely instrumental. To make Melody a competitive station in London, he would bring in more vocals and a wider range of easy listening music. He arranged a meeting with Sheila Porrit, the MD of Melody Radio, at which she offered me the breakfast show, 6–10 a.m. – which included me reading the news headlines on the hour. Now there was a challenge. The last time I had read news was in America with Thames. The studios were in Brompton Road, a very pleasant part of London, just a 20-minute drive from my home in Barnes with a private car park at the back, a nice contrast to Capital Tower on the windiest corner of London. After the hurly burly of Capital, it was more relaxing, the people were very pleasant and after my show Geoff and I would often have breakfast in the café next door. What was not to like? As Geoff's music policy took shape, Melody started building an audience. I noticed taxi drivers were listening to it, always a good sign.

Roger Moore visits Melody Radio. 007 and 006 and a half. With Melody MD Sheila Porrit

It didn't have a disco audience, of course, and I missed the contact with the public that I had always enjoyed. Out of the blue came an offer from Fulham Football Club. Would I like to host the half-time entertainment on the pitch? Another wonderful job offer, and this time just a ten-minute drive across Putney Bridge to the ground. It was a job that grew and grew. The following season, Fulham asked me if I'd like to do the match day announcing as well – announcing the teams, goal scorers and substitutes, initially from a small studio on the balcony of the famous Craven Cottage, then from the fourth official's dugout in front of the Riverside Stand from which I was so close to the play that I could hear the industrial language and feel the tackles going in. In the early days I also picked the music that was played.

I enjoyed the dark humour of the dugout. My favourite visiting manager was Stuart Pearce, then with Manchester City. After giving one of his players a severe rollicking, he strolled sheepishly over to the dugout and said, "I've tried being nice, but it doesn't work."

For me and my right-hand man, Simon Kew, our least favourite visiting manager was the one who shouted to one of his players heading into a tackle, "Break his fucking leg." I'll spare his blushes here by not mentioning his name, but within the game he is the man known as Colin.

Ray Wilkins, at one time Fulham's assistant coach, strolled into the dugout area and said to the fourth official, "Tell the referee Ray Wilkins says he's having a good game." The fourth official pressed the talkback to the ref and said, "Ray Wilkins says you're a wanker."

The next season, I was asked if after matches I would like to co-host one of the sponsors' lounges with George Cohen, Fulham's man in the England team that won the

World Cup in 1966. The expression 'Gentleman George' could have been made to fit George Cohen. A tough and fearless competitor on the football pitch, off it he was just the nicest, most decent man you could ever meet. His reading of the game was second to none and I loved his post-match analyses of the games, where we were joined by Fulham players and former colleagues of his. I was part of a group who lobbied the board to erect a statue of George outside the ground. Eventually, they agreed and George Cohen became one of the first footballers to have his statue on display while he was still alive.

In my first season as Fulham's man on the mic, the club won promotion from the Third Division where they had languished for some time, often appearing in danger of extinction. The next season, Mohamed Al Fayed joined as chairman. The Harrods boss gave the club so much money that they had the most successful run in their history. During my time as the mic man, they had two further promotions, their longest ever spell in the top division and a Europa final in Hamburg. Actually, I nearly didn't get that far with them as early in my tenure some corporate suits decided to sack me. Fayed called me up to his boardroom in Harrods, gave me my job back and a rise and promised to sack my assassins. He also gave me an envelope with some cash in it to make up for the money I'd lost by missing a game. "I don't think I should take cash from you with a name like Hamilton," I said, a reference to Neil Hamilton and the cash for questions in Parliament issue.

When I next saw the leading architect of my demise, she asked me what Fayed had said to me. I told her, "He said, 'Don't take any shit'."

It was through the meeting at Harrods that I got to know Fayed and we developed a jokey relationship. He did something I've never known a football club chairman do. Before the match I'd announce him to the crowd and he would come out and do a circuit of the pitch, twirling his black and white scarf and acknowledging their applause. He would then come over to me for a chat. I'd have to hide the microphone behind my back so the crowd couldn't hear him telling me what he would do to the team if they didn't win.

When Michael Jackson came over to open the Harrods sale, Fayed said to him, "Come and see my soccer team." Michael accepted the invitation and I was told, "Get ready to introduce Michael Jackson to the crowd." We'd had some celebrities before but no one as big as that.

On cue, I said, "Ladies and gentlemen, please welcome the one, the only Michael Jackson". When Jackson walked round the pitch with a Fulham umbrella over his head even though it was a sunny day, he did so to what I can only describe as polite applause. The crowd thought he was a lookalike. It was only when he got to the main stand that they realised he was the Michael Jackson. They didn't make the same mistake when Fayed brought along his next big star. Tony Curtis ran up the terraces and kissed some of the women.

Mohamed Al Fayed gave Fulham the greatest season in its history. After some thrilling wins at Craven Cottage against the likes of Roma and Juventus, Fulham were through to the Europa League final in Hamburg in 2010. I was asked to be there as the voice of the English announcer and to warm up the Fulham supporters on a cherry-picker high up in front of one of the stands. I've never liked heights, the cage was open at one end and both of my companions, the cherry-picker operator and a cameraman, spoke only German. I hoped they had forgotten the war. I finished my warm-up and indicated we should descend to the ground. The operator pressed a button; the cage shook but we didn't move. After a couple more attempts, I realised that we were not moving. I was cold and wet and had visions of being stuck up there, blocking the view of the crowd who were starting to shout things, like "Go forth and multiply." After what seemed like an eternity, the thing finally lowered shakily, operated, I gather, by someone on the ground. With legs shaking from both the cold and fear, I walked to my announcer's seat, smiling bravely to the Fulham supporters, just in time for kick-off. After all that, Fulham lost. But we were there.

In the early days the announcing job at Fulham was fun. There were bits of comedy I could bring to it. But

David Hamilton
at
Variety Club Day
-
Sandown Park
-
Saturday
20th August 2005

as the club became more successful, it became more corporate and more serious. I always liked to be courteous to visiting supporters. When Norwich were relegated after a match at our ground, I mentioned how wonderful their supporters were – which was true – and how we looked forward to welcoming them back when they returned soon to the Premier League. This apparently was why some of the suits wanted to get rid of me. They wanted to turn the place into Fortress Fulham, a place where people feared to come. This was never the ethos of Fulham, a unique club because of its setting and the type of supporters it has always attracted. The suits wanted it to be more tribal.

On May 21, 2009, *Match of the Day* ran a feature on me and my touchline role. As luck would have it that day, Manchester United were the visitors, Wayne Rooney and Paul Scholes were sent off and Fulham won 2-nil. I couldn't have had a better day for my cameo. Sir Alex Ferguson wasn't a very happy bunny. Apparently, with its cramped dressing room in the Cottage, Fulham wasn't his favourite ground.

It certainly wasn't on that day.

Every time I said I was going to pack it in, Fayed offered me more money. When he left, I decided to go as well. After my final match, Fulham presented me with a crystal football on a plinth with the inscription: 'David Hamilton, FFC, 18 Glorious Years'.

There was an old-time actor and TV presenter called Jerry Desmonde, who said of show business, "One door closes, another closes." While I understand what he meant, I've been lucky to find that isn't always the case. Soon after I quit my job at Fulham, I was asked to compere a show at the London Palladium featuring a band called The Fugitives, plus a boy and two girl singers. They were a great band and nice guys to work with, and after the show they suggested we did more shows together. Thus at the age of 77 I embarked on a 50-theatre tour they called 'David Hamilton's Rock 'n' Roll Back The Years'. On stage I told little stories behind the music and enjoyed banter with the band. During rehearsals they suggested I sing in the finale. I was a little nervous about this, partly because I was worried I might forget the words. After a couple of shows I started to really enjoy it. During the rock 'n' roll medley I would change in the wings into my gold lamé suit, then leap on stage and sing 'Great Balls Of Fire'.

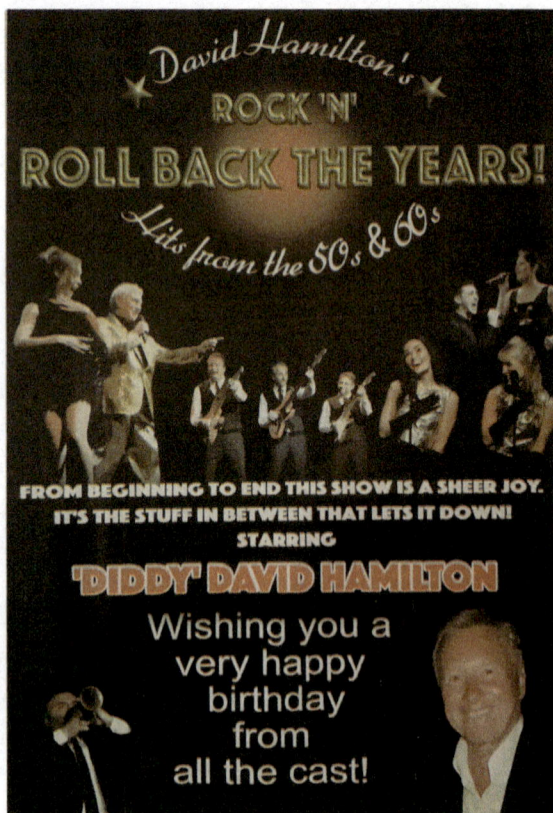

David Hamilton's
★ ROCK 'N' ★
ROLL BACK THE YEARS!
Hits from the 50s & 60s

FROM BEGINNING TO END THIS SHOW IS A SHEER JOY.
IT'S THE STUFF IN BETWEEN THAT LETS IT DOWN!
STARRING
'DIDDY' DAVID HAMILTON

Wishing you a very happy birthday from all the cast!

After the tour I was working on a cruise. In an interview on stage with the entertainments director I mentioned the tour and my singing.

"We'd like to hear that, wouldn't we?" she said to the audience, who all cheered. "You could sing with our band."

I protested that I'd only ever sung with one band, but she'd have nothing of it and insisted I rehearse with her band and sing on the last night of the cruise. When I rehearsed with the band the next afternoon, it was dreadful. I sounded like a strangled cat. Even to my untrained ear it was clear that the band and I were in different keys. "You sing in B flat," said the bandleader. This was not music to my ears. "Oh, it's OK. We can play in B flat."

On the last night I was so nervous I couldn't eat my dinner. But again when I got up on stage I really enjoyed it. So much so that I segued into 'Hi Ho Silver Lining'. The start of a singing career? I fear not. A bit late in the day for that.

Leo Sayer borrows my gold jacket and doesn't want to give it back

CHAPTER 22

Back to the Farm

I'D always had Minis since the sixties, such great little cars. They were ideal for London where you could leave them on half a parking place. I often walked past the London Mini Centre half a mile from my home and thought I should buy one. What prompted me to do so was hearing that the number plate D1 DDY was available in a DVLA sale in Preston. I had someone bid for it on my behalf. I got it and put it on a red Mini which I called the Diddymobile. It fitted nicely into the parking space at Melody Radio.

With the Diddymobile

When Lord Hanson sold Melody to Emap for £25 million (it having made a profit of £500,000 in the previous year) I knew that I, as the host of the breakfast show and the highest paid presenter, would be the most vulnerable. I was right. Luckily, I was offered some shows by another station just a few hundred yards further up the Brompton Road. Liberty Radio was owned by Mohamed Al Fayed and carried commentaries of Fulham matches so that was a good fit. As part of the deal I was allowed free parking in Harrods car park. One day I saw someone taking a close look at my car. It was Didier Deschamps, the Chelsea footballer.

"I like your number plate," he said. "It is my name."

"It's my name as well," I said, without going into explanation.

"How much you want for it?" he enquired.

"Twenty thousand," I said.

"Only?"

Realising I was talking to a top footballer who was earning £40,000 a week, I hurriedly said, "And another twenty for the one on the back."

Sadly, not long after our conversation Didier was transferred from Chelsea to Valencia and I never did sell him my plate. A decent profit from a Chelsea player would have been nice.

Liberty Radio didn't last too long. Mohamed Al Fayed had bought it for his son as part of his media empire. When Dodi died he lost interest in it and sold it to the Universal Church of the Kingdom of God – so no work there.

I was still doing some shows for Classic Gold, a group of AM stations whose studios were in Dunstable, when thankfully another offer came along. Saga, the organisation that catered for the over 50s, was interested in radio and was building some studios in Buckingham Gate, just around the corner from the Palace. They had appointed Ron Coles, an experienced radio man, to run their radio division. I had only met Ron once briefly at a radio event, but he offered me a daily show on Prime Time Radio, one of the early digital stations.

Under Ron's guidance, the Saga Radio empire grew at a fast pace. A year after the launch of Prime Time, Saga won the licence for an FM station covering the West Midlands. Ron asked me to do the breakfast show, Monday to Friday. This launched me into a broadcasting marathon. On Sunday nights I would drive up to Birmingham where Saga booked me into the Plough and Harrow Hotel in Hagley Road, next door to their studios. I would then do the breakfast show on Saga FM West Midlands, 6–9 a.m., have breakfast at the hotel, do the Prime Time show live from 10 a.m.–1 p.m. and then record a daily show for Saga Radio's national station on DAB – i.e. seven hours' broadcasting, five days a week.

Saga then won a licence to broadcast to the East Midlands, so after 15 months in Birmingham I moved to Nottingham for a similar schedule but at different times: Prime Time live 9 a.m.–12 p.m.; lunch break; Saga FM East Midlands live, 1–4 p.m.; 4 p.m., record Saga Radio national shows. This time an extra show was thrown into the mix. One night a week at Walton's Hotel in Nottingham I would research and write the 'Million Sellers', which I would then record on Wednesday afternoon. Total broadcasting, 37 hours a week.

Saga Radio was on a roll and won another licence, this time for Glasgow. I was due to go there next until a bombshell dropped. We were all called in to a meeting in the office at the Nottingham studio to be told that Roger De Haan was selling Saga, the family business his father had set up years before. The people who bought it weren't interested in radio and the whole radio division was sold off to the Guardian Media Group who re-branded it without the Saga name. That didn't stop us all traipsing down to London to receive Prime Time's award of digital station of the year.

Dreena, David and Max

While I was in Nottingham the Hamilton household acquired a new dog. After Rosie died there was a considerable period of mourning. We'd resisted several overtures to take in a rescue dog but eventually we succumbed. Max was a liver and tan Gordon Setter (unusual colour because most are black and tan). He was driven down from Edinburgh where he'd been a regimental mascot. While with the Army he'd been run over by a lorry and two of his legs had been pinned. It's likely that he had some brain damage, too, because he was certainly eccentric. He arrived in a large cage which he seemed to have spent a lot of time in. He was obsessed with mirrors and flashing lights. Basically, he was barking. Where Rosie was an angel, he was a rascal. But a lovable one.

Max was a big, magnificent-looking dog who attracted attention wherever he went. On walks in Richmond Park people would ask, "What breed is he?" and say, "Isn't he handsome?" Unfortunately, he was wild and would often go missing. One day in the park I lost him for an hour and a half. There was an eerie silence and I feared the worst. Then out of the blue he came back to me. Another time he rounded up about 300 deer and moved them from one side of the park to another, including across two roads. There were all these deer, twice as big as him, and he chased them all. How we didn't get banned from the park is a mystery. How he survived is another. On his walks he seemed to have a liking for neutered males. I wondered if he was a Gay Gordon.

At home he would watch football on television with me. When the ball went behind the goal he'd go round the back of the television to try to find it. I joked that, knowing my luck, he was probably a Chelsea supporter. He was Mad Max, for sure. So much so that Dreena put him up for the TV show, *It's Me or the Dog*. Victoria Stilwell came to the house and filmed some of his eccentricities. We then went to Richmond Park.

The director told me, "Stop in the car park. Let him out of the boot and we'll film him running around the park." I did all that. Max jumped out of the car, ran towards a family nearby and peed all over their picnic. The crew apologised profusely, but quietly were in stitches. "Does he always do that?" asked the director.

"He's never done it before," I said. "He's probably playing up for the camera."

We walked him round the grounds of Amberley Castle. There was a sign saying DOGS MUST NOT FOUL ON

THE GRASS. He crapped all over the sign. *It's Me or the Dog* was shown over and over again on television. The episode with Max is now one of the most viewed on YouTube.

In 2005 I was compering a show at Dubai Country Club that starred The Foundations, Dave Dee and Marmalade, the first Scottish band to have a UK number 1, which they did with Paul McCartney's song 'OB LA DI OB LA DA'. Over dinner before the show I asked if anyone had seen Junior Campbell, former member of Marmalade who I used to play football with in the Showbiz XI. Dave Dee said, "He lives on a remote farm in Sussex. You go down a narrow, twisting road until you get to a farm track. It's a very old house by a river and a mill. You'd never find it."

It sounded very much like the farm I grew up on. There couldn't be too many places that match that description. I took Junior's number and resolved to phone him when I got back to the UK.

Junior said, "Yes, the farmer said you used to live here. Why don't you come down and have lunch with me and Susie?"

So we took the long and winding road back to the farm I hadn't seen since I was 15. It all came back to me. Still there was the farmhouse where I kicked a football against the wall, smashing the window and running away in shame. Junior and Susie were living in what had been a dilapidated cottage where Daisy, the land girl, had stored potatoes, now restored into a Grade 2 listed home. We had a lovely lunch in the sunshine beside the swimming pool. It was enchanting.

"If you ever sell it, you must let me know," I said.

A year later, Junior phoned me. "Just to let you

know, we're moving on. We're putting the house on the market."

"Don't do that," I said. "I'll buy it and save you the agency fee."

So I bought the house for the asking price. For a couple of years we had it as a weekend retreat or holiday home. Then a big contract came to an end and we made the decision to sell the house in Barnes and move to Sussex full-time.

It was sad to be leaving Barnes, as we'd made some good friends there. It was on a dog walk on Barnes Common that we met Annie, wife of the actor Derek Bond. Derek was the handsome star of many movies. He played Oates in *Scott of the Antarctic*. Who could forget the scene where he walked off into the blizzard to save his crew mates, saying, "I'm just going outside and may be some time"? While we were neighbours we re-united Derek with his co-star from the film, John Mills, who he hadn't seen for many years.

Derek and Annie were wonderful party givers and the great thing was they were within staggering distance of our home, just a few doors away. New Year's Eves were particularly memorable, with some of Derek's actor friends including Trevor Bannister (from *Are You Being Served?*) with his wife Pammy, Annie and Peter Gilmore, who met on *The Onedin Line*, and the wonderful June Whitfield. June and I sang 'If You Were the Only Girl/Boy in the World'. We sang it again when I got the last radio interview with her at her care home in Kingston, just days before she passed away.

Max the dog loved Sussex and gave a happy howl every time he came here. Not surprising. I walked him over the fields where I'd walked with Scamp when I was a little boy and over every other walking path we could find within miles.

Holiday time with Dreena

Somehow or other Daisy got in touch and came to visit us with her family, the first time she'd been here since the war. Though she was in her nineties, her long-term recall was marvellous. She remembered things about my mother and my grandparents and how kind they were when she was seconded to them during the war and lived in a cottage nearby. I reminded her of the time as a young boy when I mischievously dumped some field mice down her blouse. "Yes, and don't do it again," she said.

During her visit, I was opening a local fête, and she came along and was photographed with me in the *West Sussex County Times*. The newspaper was also there when I opened the summer fête at Horsham Hospital where I'd had my tonsils removed when I was five or six. "I've come to get them back," I told the crowd.

The *West Sussex County Times* had history for me, as my father worked there when he met my mother. When

Gary Shipton, the Editor, discovered this, he gave me a tour of the offices. My father would have appreciated the fact that there was a pub next door.

The farm has always been a magnet for people. Townies loved to drive down here, some using it as halfway house en route to the coast. One day we found a little old lady walking down the farm lane with a young man. We discovered he was her grandson who had brought her there. It turned out to be my Uncle John's daughter, Win. She was surprised when she found out that John's nephew was living here. We invited them to join us for tea in the garden where we talked about John. It was priceless talking to Daisy and Win. Outside of my first wife and my son and daughter, they were the only people who remembered my parents and my Uncle John and they alone remembered my grandparents. Sadly, both did not live long after their visits here.

Nor, alas, did Max. He had had a long history of health problems. He cost us a fortune in vets' bills. Unlike Rosie, he didn't have a long life. We nursed him through as long as we could but he died at 10. Despite all his problems, we wouldn't have missed a moment of Mad Max. Thanks for all the laughs, Maxy boy.

I think if we had had him from a puppy, things might have been different, but the first eighteen months of his life had been very difficult. When we lost him, I thought we might in time find a female liver and tan Gordon, but one day Dreena went to Wales with her daughter Charlotte, who was looking for a Cocker Spaniel. Something told me that Dreena would come back with one as well. Sure enough, when I got back that night from a gig there was newspaper all over the kitchen floor. Charlotte had bought a pedigree Cocker and Dreena had come back with the runt from the litter. Buy one, get one free.

Charlotte called hers Dolly and we called ours Amber, which is her colour. Like Rosie and Max, she's appeared with me in newspapers and magazines. Dolly and Amber are now old ladies. How quickly time flies. It's wonderful for children to grow up with dogs. The only downside is that their lives are so short and they break your heart when they go.

CHAPTER 23

Broadcasting from the Farm

S INCE leaving Radio 2 in 1986, I've spent the best part of 40 years in commercial radio. It's radio, but not as I knew it. At the BBC we complained they weren't businesslike and they were up against people who were. In commercial radio it's all business, where the sales team are as important as the presenters, if not more so. When I jumped ship to Radio 210 at the age of 48, I went to a station that was a prime example of how local radio should work – supplying listeners with local news, travel, sport and weather with a strong sense of community. I could never have guessed that in a few years it would be the subject of a merger and then part of a national network. No long-term future there. Likewise the stations at Swindon and Peterborough.

Capital Gold and Classic Gold got rid of their name presenters and became virtually an all-day juke box. Melody became part of the Magic network. When Saga Radio folded they were bombarded with emails from over-50s who'd bought DAB radios, only to find there was no station catering for their interests. Mike Read invited me to join him at Big L, a tribute to Radio London, based in Frinton-on-Sea. I spent a year in Frinton, a gem on the Essex coast. Mike organised a celebrity tennis tournament which I played in at the town's wonderful tennis club. I wouldn't have missed my year in Frinton, but the station had a weak AM single and very few people in the early 2000s were listening to radio online.

Age UK decided to go into radio, no doubt spotting the gap left by Saga, and launched a station, aptly called The Wireless. Rob Jones, who was running it, invited me to do a daily show, seven days a week. Because I couldn't travel to and from London every day and because budgets were tight, I took the train up once a fortnight and recorded 14 four-hour shows in a day. Another broadcasting marathon. Most of the listeners were in Age UK shops around the country, hence the feature 'Shop of the Day'. After seven years, a new CEO joined Age UK and decided they didn't want to be in radio any more. Another one bites the dust.

Shaun Tilley is a young broadcaster whose potential I had spotted early in his career when he invited me to do some recordings in Liverpool. By the 2000s he was running KC FM in Hull and persuaded Tony Blackburn, Ed Stewart, Paul Burnett and me to do some shows up there. It was good to get together with the boys, but guess what? KC FM is now part of a big group. For a while Shaun was an agent and suggested I did some shows for BBC local radio. So I stood in for a holidaying Judi Spiers at BBC Radio Devon, first in Plymouth and then Exeter. Sometimes Dreena would come with me and after the show was finished we'd walk Amber along some of the lovely Devon beaches. Such a beautiful part of the country. Working for the BBC again was like going home. Unlike commercial radio stations, whose studios were often on trading estates, the Beeb's are mostly in lovely old houses in smart areas. Every time I went to Radio Devon, the programme controller Mark Grinnell would take me and the production team out for lunch, a nice touch. One day he asked me if I would consider re-locating and joining them full-time. It was tempting but I had not long ago re-located to Sussex and I still had my job at Fulham. Just as well I didn't take up his offer when I see what is happening at BBC local radio now and their cull of broadcasters over 60 and people having to re-apply for their jobs. How degrading. It did lead to me doing shows for my local station, BBC Radio Sussex and Surrey in both Brighton and Guildford and occasionally for BBC Radio Solent in Southampton. I've now broadcast from just about every big town and city in the UK. The one place I'd never broadcast from was my home.

David and Dreena, Patrons of Rangers Lodge Wildlife Hospital near Horsham with owners Russ and Jane Burrows.

I did do some television shows from home. Gloria Hunniford, my old colleague from Radio 2 days, came to my Sussex home for *Cash in the Celebrity Attic*, where I was able to raise £5000 for the Roy Castle Cancer Fund. Lisa Snowdon came here when I was a guest on *Through the Keyhole*, having done the show twice while I was in Barnes. Actually, the Barnes shows were particular fun because I had a DJ's loo that Lloyd Grossman was fascinated by. The idea had come to me to cover the walls with picture discs. I had everyone from Madonna to Marilyn Monroe, Bing Crosby with White Christmas to Earth, Wind and Fire. Friends would see it and add some of their own. The mirror was a reproduction of the Rolling Stones hot lips logo and outside the loo was a sign that lit up when someone closed the door. It read: 'ON AIR'. Lloyd Grossman was filmed sitting on the loo saying, "Who would have a lavatory like this?"

I didn't do *Strictly* because I'm no dancer, but I did do *Let's Dance for Sports Relief* with Tony Blackburn, where we danced, if that's the word, to 'Push It' by Salt 'n' Pepper. It entailed a week of rehearsals at Elstree. Halfway through the week we met the costumes lady who started talking about skirts and earrings. It was only then that we realised we were going to do it as girls. We thought we were going to do it as Tony Blackburn and David Hamilton. Altogether more gentle was *Celebrity Road Trip* with Kate Silverton, where we went to Newark, Nottingham and Derby, although even that had a sting in the tail. I was several miles down the motorway, quite tired after three days of filming, when I realised I was still wearing the microphone. A quick about turn, back to Derby, where luckily the crew were still there.

I did *Pointless Celebrities* (very apt) twice, first with Tony Blackburn, then with Jenny Hanley. I was due to do it a third time with Anne Diamond when Covid struck. I'd had lots of contact with the BBC about the precautions they would take at the Elstree studios. No green room. Masks to be worn at all times except in the studio. Leave dressing room doors open so no one touches the handles. The list was endless. The day before the recording was due, my agent phoned me. My appearance had been cancelled. Because of my age (over 80), they couldn't get health insurance for me.

"That's it," I said to Dreena on a walk with Amber. "It's all over. The game's up." I could see Covid finishing my 60-year career.

"It's not over until the fat lady sings," she said.

A few weeks later I got a call from David Lloyd, a highly experienced radio man who I'd worked with at Saga Radio in Nottingham. The last time I'd spoken to David was when he interviewed me for a podcast he was doing while I was on my rock 'n' roll tour. I had played Derby the night before and booked into Waltons Hotel in Nottingham, where I had stayed during my year with Saga. David turned up with a tape recorder after breakfast. He later sent me a copy of the recording that finished with some beautiful music. It sounded a bit like an obituary. I remember one thing I said about my career: I felt I should have done more.

Well, now here was the chance. David was on the phone, telling me he was setting up a new radio station for boomers. He was going to call it Boom Radio. Because of the pandemic everyone would be broadcasting from home. Did I want to be involved? You bet I did, but I told him I didn't have a home studio. "We'll build you one," he said. Within a few days, pieces of equipment started to arrive – a microphone, headphones and a new computer that stored all the music. Peter Monnery, a producer I'd worked with at the BBC, came round to install it all and a few weeks before launch I did a few trial runs to get the hang of it.

David kindly gave me the lunchtime show from 12 to 2, a very civilised time that gave me the chance to have breakfast and go through the morning papers. Boom Radio launched on Valentine's Day, 2021, with a line-up that included radio veterans like Graham Dene, Nicky Horne and Roger Day. I started off broadcasting from a shed in the garden but by the next winter I'd moved to an attic upstairs – much more friendly on cold mornings.

In the Boom Radio studio

Boom Radio was an instant success, attracting lots of disaffected listeners from Radio 2, which was now aiming for a younger audience. Unlike so many stations that played the same small bunch of records over and over again because a panel said they were safe, Boom built up a huge playlist, over 15,000 records and rising. Based on the experience of David Lloyd and his music man Paul Robey, they knew that listeners loved a record that came as a surprise, something perhaps they hadn't heard for years.

Boom launched with five or six DAB outlets in major UK cities. Within a month the reaction was such that a decision was made to go national.

Radio stations live or die by RAJARS, the quarterly listening figures that tell them how they are doing. Every-one has known bad ones; jobs have been lost because of them. So far Boom's have soared. Working on a small budget compared with the giants of the industry like Global and Bauer, much of it has been done by word of mouth. I can't remember a station where there has been such great feedback.

Without Boom, I would probably have eased into a gentle retirement. As it was, at the age of 82 I was enjoying a new lease of life. Now 70s TV booked me for some shows, which I recorded at home during lockdown. There were talking heads shows for Channel 5 on every subject from music to Ken Dodd and Tommy Cooper to the Winter of Discontent. GB News invited me in to do newspaper reviews.

It had taken a long time, but 35 years after leaving Radio 2 I was back on national radio again. Not only that, but I was the oldest broadcaster doing a national daily show.

Knowing the right time to quit is a difficult conundrum. I gave up my job at Thames because I felt I'd been doing it long enough. I finished at Fulham because I was starting to freeze on winter days in the dugout, I was having trouble spotting the goal scorers and I didn't want to make mistakes. Walking out of Radio 2 because I knew we were playing the wrong music was probably the hardest decision I had to make and took me from national to local radio overnight. Would I have lasted there many more years and gone on and on like Ken Bruce and Steve Wright? Probably not, with the management of the time. Station closures, mergers and changes of management are all the enemies of the freelance broadcaster. Managers always bring in new people because they get no credit from the success of presenters they've inherited. It's hard to last a lifetime in a business like ours. Well over 20 of the radio and TV stations I've worked for are now gone.

I did have a go at running a couple of stations. I was a director at Lite FM in Peterborough where I made the mistake of taking a salary instead of having an investment in the company. Thus when it was sold I made no money. Armed with that experience, I did become an investor in Splash FM in Worthing where I did the launch programme with the guest, local boy Leo Sayer. Splash in time became the subject of a merger and is now part of the More Radio group. The brutal truth is that all these local radio stations only make serious money when they are sold. When that happens, a lot of people lose their jobs. As well as the loss of income, the people who feel that most are the ones who live and breathe their station and put all their efforts into making it a success.

CHAPTER 24

Home at Last

NINE months into my new job with Boom I found myself peeing blood one morning. After a blood test at my local GP's surgery, I was told to report to Hazlemere Hospital where X-rays showed I had an enlarged prostate, nothing unusual for someone my age, but something to keep an eye on. But there was also a condition that was more sinister. I was told I had too many red blood cells. This didn't surprise me, I joked. I always knew I was too red-blooded. When Dreena and I arrived at St Luke's Hospital in Guildford I realised there was nothing to joke about.

"This is a cancer hospital," I said to her. "What am I doing here? I haven't got cancer. I've got too many red blood cells."

Sadly, it turned out that I had a condition called poly-cythaemia vera, which is a cancer of the blood. As I understand it, too many red cells mean the blood is thick and takes time to pump around the body. This could lead to a heart attack or a stroke. To try to prevent this happening, once a week I had to report to St Luke's for a procedure called venesection, which involved taking a bag of blood (a pint) from me. This proved difficult, as my veins seemed to have disappeared. After several attempts to find a vein, the nurses would sometimes get only half a bag, on one occasion only a quarter. It was a slow process, which I felt could be as traumatic for them as it was for me. So I tried to make light of it. "You can't get blood out of a stone," I said to the nurses. "Ask my wife, she should know."

Having been blessed with 80 years of wonderful health, my only experience of hospitals had been when I had my tonsils removed as a boy and when I had my car crash and wound up in Leeds Infirmary. I was always squeamish about needles and blood tests and now I was having a lot of them, and even they were not easy. On venesection days I'd come out of the ward with my shirt wringing wet.

Luckily, I've had a wonderful consultant at St Luke's. Knowing how difficult giving blood is for me, she's put me on chemotherapy pills which seem to be doing the trick. The only side-effect from them seems to be that at times I get tired. What I have is not curable – I've got it forever – but hopefully it is manageable.

As I write, I'm now in my mid-80s and have outlived my parents by nearly 30 years. How I've done it is a

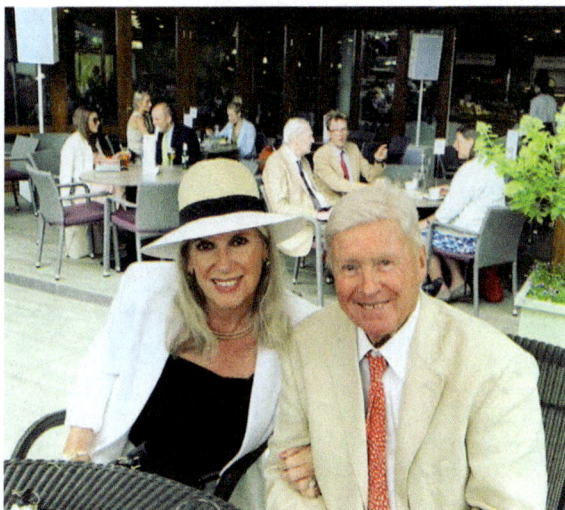

Dreena and me at Wimbledon, 2023

mystery. With the life I've lived I should have burned out years ago. I can look back on over 13,000 radio shows I've hosted, over 1,000 TV shows, 1,000 club appearances and 1,000 openings of various events and businesses. For some time I was doing 50,000 miles a year on the road. My work rate is such that there's no doubt some of my relationships have suffered because of it. But my children and step-children are all talking to me and so are my grandchildren and step-grandchildren. Between us, Dreena and I have five children and nine grandchildren. My daughter Jane is a teacher; my son David junior a journalist. Dreena's three, Angela, Simon and Charlotte, are doing well, too. Everyone has picked up the work ethic and, what is more, they're all decent people I can be proud of, and so are their children.

Dreena and I have been together now for 40 years. How she has put up with me and my showbusiness ego for all that time is another mystery. She is the wind beneath my wings.

Four of our (grown up) kids. Simon, Jane, Charlotte and Angela

Party time for my son and daughter with Debbie and Tony Blackburn and Julie, wife of Graham Dene

I count myself a very lucky man to have found a job I've loved for 60-plus years. I thank the people who gave me the vital breaks in the early days. Without them I might have been the gang boss Mr Hawkins predicted. I thank my broadcasting hero, Pete Murray, for his inspiration which led me to a life-long career. In time my hero became my friend. For Christmas 2022, I recorded a

Pete Murray, at age 97, chats to me on Boom Radio
Photo: Emilie Sandy

two-hour show with him for Boom at his home in Wimbledon. At the age of 97 he was as bright and witty as ever and his recall of his life was incredible.

When I started impersonating the people on the wireless as a boy on that remote farm I would never have guessed that one day it would be a broadcasting hub from which I, too, would be speaking to the nation on the radio. The long and winding road had finally brought me back. I was home at last.

Epilogue

A wee story to end on.

When I was a teenager I went to see the wonderful comedian Max Miller at the Chiswick Empire. He was known as the 'Cheeky Chappie', famous for his *double-entendres* and risqué jokes from his blue book. He was once banned by BBC radio for doing a joke that was far too rude to repeat here. Without doubt he inspired many stand-up comics who came along in his wake.

Somebody told me a story about Max Miller that I have never forgotten. Val Parnell took a risk when he booked Max for the Royal Variety Performance in 1950. Val was a very powerful man, boss of Moss Empires which controlled most of the major theatres in the country, later becoming joint managing director of ATV. For variety acts, if you didn't work for Val, you didn't work. It was as simple as that.

Before the Royal Variety Show, Val gave Max two instructions. "The Royal family are in, so nothing from the blue book. Keep it clean. The other thing is – Jack Benny is the top comic and will close the show. You are the second comic and will do six minutes, not a minute more."

Max was dismayed that six minutes was not long enough for him to make an impact and angry that Jack Benny had been given twenty minutes.

Once he got on stage the audience loved him. He did nothing from the blue book, the royal box was rocking with laughter. There was so much laughter and applause that the act spread to twelve minutes, with the result that Jack Benny had to cut his act short. Val Parnell was furious. He stormed into Max's dressing room, shouting, "I told you to do six minutes and you did twelve. You can't work to orders. You will never work for me again. You're finished."

Max Miller stood up, put on his hat and his overcoat and said, "Val, you're a million pounds too late." With that, he left the theatre and caught the train home to Brighton. The next day everybody was talking, not about Jack Benny but about Max Miller, who'd been a sensation the night before.

Our business is notoriously fickle. Artists can go out of fashion and disappear overnight. I was once told there are four stages of show business:

"Who's Fred Bloggs?"

"Get me Fred Bloggs."

"Get me a younger version of Fred Bloggs."

"Who's Fred Bloggs?"

Max Miller understood how the business worked. His story was an inspiration to us all.

OUTRO

IN 1989, thirty years after my time with the British Forces Network in Germany, I was invited back to do an anniversary show for them in Cologne. Not long afterwards BFN – by now known as BFBS, the British Forces Broadcasting Service – moved out of Cologne. Its two buildings were sold off to developers who promptly demolished them. When the bulldozers moved in, they found in the garden where we used to play football an unexploded British World War II bomb.

If we'd set that off while we were kicking a ball around, what an own goal that would have been.

Reflecting on life with Amber behind me. Always some cracks on the long and winding road of life, even if under Mr Blue Sky. (Photo: Peter Robertson)

Contracts

Tyne-Tees Television: 1961–62

ABC Television: 1962–68

Thames Television: 1968–1980

BBC Light Programme: 1967–68

BBC Radio 1 and 2: 1967–1986

Radio 210: 1987–88

TVS *All Clued Up*: 1989–1992

Lifestyle TV: 1985–1993

Capital Gold: 1988–1994

Melody Radio: 1995–1998

Liberty Radio: 1998–2000

Classic Gold: 1999–2002

PrimeTime Radio: 2000–2006

Big L Radio: 2006–2008

Fulham FC matchday MC: 1996–2014

The Wireless: 2012–2018

Boom Radio: 2021–

Index of Names

Printed in Great Britain
by Amazon